Fast and Easy

AIR FRYER

Cookbook With Pictures

Simple, Healthy, and Deliciously Diverse Air Fryer Recipes for Beginners | Everyday Gourmet with Full Color Pictures 2024 Editions.

Jamie Culinary

TABLE OF CONTENTS

Warning-Disclaimer

This book is intended to provide both educational content and entertainment. The author or publisher does not provide any assurance of success for those who implement the techniques, suggestions, tips, ideas, or strategies contained within. The author and publisher disclaim liability for any loss or damage, direct or indirect, that may be incurred through the application of the information provided in this book.

Introduction

Welcome to a culinary adventure that promises to redefine the way you think about cooking! Our air fryer cookbook is not just a collection of recipes; it's a gateway to a world of flavors, textures, and aromas, all achieved with the marvel of air frying technology.

Air frying has revolutionized the kitchen, offering a healthier, quicker, and more energy-efficient method of cooking. This magical appliance circulates hot air around the food, resulting in dishes that are crispy on the outside and tender on the inside, with a fraction of the oil used in traditional frying methods. Whether you're a seasoned chef or a novice in the kitchen, this cookbook will guide you through an array of dishes that will tantalize your taste buds and impress your loved ones.

In these pages, you'll find recipes ranging from classic comfort foods to innovative dishes that will inspire your culinary creativity. We'll explore the versatility of the air fryer, showing you how it can be used for more than just frying – think baking, roasting, and even grilling. Each recipe is designed to be straightforward and fuss-free, ensuring you spend less time in the kitchen and more time enjoying your delicious creations.

Our journey will also include tips and tricks to get the most out of your air fryer, as well as advice on choosing the right ingredients and making healthy eating a delightful experience. Whether you're looking to whip up quick weeknight dinners, prepare impressive meals for special occasions, or explore new culinary horizons, this cookbook is your trusted companion.

So, let's turn the page and begin this exciting journey together. Embrace the simplicity, indulge in the flavors, and transform the way you cook with our Air Fryer Cookbook. Happy air frying!

Getting Started with Your Air Fryer

Welcome to the beginning of your air frying journey! Before we dive into the delicious recipes awaiting you, let's get acquainted with the fundamentals of air frying. This section is designed to help you understand your air fryer, its capabilities, and how to use it safely and effectively.

1. Understanding Your Air Fryer:
An air fryer is a compact, countertop appliance that cooks by circulating hot air around food. It mimics the results of deep-frying with significantly less oil, offering a healthier alternative. Most air fryers are equipped with a basket to place food in, a temperature control, and a timer. Familiarize yourself with your specific model's features and instructions.

2. Setting Up:
Choose a safe location for your air fryer on a flat, heat-resistant surface. Ensure it's away from any overhead cabinets to allow for proper air circulation. Before the first use, run your air fryer empty for a few minutes to remove any residual odors or manufacturing oils.

3. Preheating:
Many recipes benefit from preheating the air fryer, which typically takes about 3-5 minutes. Refer to your air fryer's manual for specific preheating instructions.

4. Cooking and Safety Tips:

Spacing: Avoid overcrowding the basket. Air needs to circulate around the food for even cooking and crispiness.
Shaking or Flipping: For even cooking, shake the basket or flip the food halfway through cooking, especially for items like fries or vegetables.
Oil Use: While air frying requires less oil, a light spray or toss in oil can enhance texture and flavor, especially for vegetables or lean meats.
Temperature and Timing: Air fryers cook faster than traditional ovens. Start with lower cooking times and temperatures and adjust as needed.
Cleaning: Regular cleaning is important. Ensure the appliance is cool before cleaning. Most baskets and trays are dishwasher safe, but check your manual for specific instructions.

5. Experiment and Enjoy:
Each air fryer is unique, so don't hesitate to experiment with cooking times and temperatures to find what works best for your model and your taste preferences. Remember, cooking is an adventure!

6. Additional Accessories:
Consider investing in air fryer accessories like parchment liners or additional racks, which can expand your cooking options and make cleanup easier.

As you start your air frying adventure, remember that patience and practice are key. Every recipe is an opportunity to learn and refine your skills. Now that you're equipped with the basics, let's turn up the heat and start cooking!

Tips and Tricks for Mastering Air Frying

Air frying is more than just a healthier alternative to traditional frying; it's a versatile and convenient cooking method. To help you get the most out of your air fryer, here are some tips and tricks that will elevate your air frying game:

Preheat for Perfection: Just like a conventional oven, preheating your air fryer can lead to better cooking results. It ensures immediate high heat, which is key for achieving that desirable crispy texture.

Don't Overcrowd: To ensure even cooking, avoid overcrowding the basket. Air needs to circulate around the food. Cooking in batches might take longer, but the results are worth it.

Shake or Flip Regularly: For items like French fries, veggies, or small chicken wings, shaking the basket periodically ensures even cooking and browning. For larger items, flipping halfway through cooking is essential.

Use a Light Oil Spray: A little oil goes a long way in an air fryer. Use a light spray of oil on foods that you want to be extra crispy. Opt for oils with a high smoke point, like canola or avocado oil.

Keep It Dry: Pat foods dry before cooking. Removing excess moisture helps achieve a crispy finish, especially for marinated meats or washed vegetables.

Baking in the Air Fryer: Your air fryer can bake too! For best results, reduce your usual oven temperature by 25°F and start checking for doneness a little earlier than the recipe suggests.

Layering and Racks: If your air fryer comes with racks, use them to cook multiple layers of food, like vegetables and meat, simultaneously. Just remember to switch the racks halfway through cooking for even results.

Aluminum Foil and Parchment Paper: These can be used in an air fryer for easier cleanup or to prevent smaller items from falling through the basket. However, ensure they don't cover the entire bottom to allow for proper air circulation.

Resting Time for Meats: After air frying, let meats rest for a few minutes before cutting. This allows the juices to redistribute, ensuring your meat is juicy and tender.

Keep It Clean: Regular cleaning not only prolongs the life of your air fryer but also prevents flavors from previous meals from transferring to your next dish. Check your manual for specific cleaning instructions.

Remember, every air fryer is unique, and practice makes perfect. These tips and tricks are starting points for exploration and innovation in your air frying journey. Experiment, adjust, and most importantly, have fun with your cooking!

Chapter 1: Breakfast

Air Fryer Elote Avocado Toast

Prep: 10 mins | Cook: 8 mins | Serves 2

Ingredients:

- 2 large slices of sourdough bread
- 1 ripe avocado
- 1 ear of corn
- 1 tablespoon olive oil
- 1/2 teaspoon chili powder
- Salt to taste
- 2 tablespoons cotija cheese, crumbled
- 1 tablespoon fresh cilantro, chopped
- 1 lime, cut into wedges

Instructions:

1. Preheat the air fryer to 375°F (190°C).
2. Brush the ear of corn with olive oil and sprinkle with chili powder and a pinch of salt.
3. Place the corn in the air fryer basket and cook for 8 minutes, turning halfway through until the kernels are slightly charred.
4. While the corn is cooking, mash the avocado in a bowl and season with salt.
5. Toast the sourdough bread in the air fryer for 3 minutes or until it reaches your desired crispness.
6. Once the corn is done, let it cool for a minute before slicing the kernels off the cob.
7. Spread the mashed avocado evenly on the toasted sourdough slices.
8. Top with the air-fried corn kernels, crumbled cotija cheese, and chopped cilantro.
9. Serve with lime wedges for squeezing over the top.

Cooking Tips:

- For a creamier avocado spread, mix in a tablespoon of Greek yogurt.
- You can add a pinch of smoked paprika to the corn for extra smokiness.

Air Fryer French Toast Sticks

Prep: 10 mins | Cook: 10 mins | Serves 4

Ingredients:

- 8 slices of thick-cut bread, cut into sticks
- 2 large eggs
- 1/2 cup milk
- 2 tablespoons sugar
- 1 teaspoon vanilla extract
- 1 teaspoon ground cinnamon
- Butter or non-stick cooking spray for greasing

Instructions:

1. Preheat the air fryer to 360°F (182°C).
2. In a shallow dish, whisk together eggs, milk, sugar, vanilla extract, and cinnamon.
3. Dip each bread stick into the egg mixture, allowing the excess to drip off.
4. Grease the air fryer basket with butter or non-stick cooking spray.
5. Place the coated bread sticks in the basket in a single layer, making sure they are not touching.
6. Cook for 5 minutes, then flip the sticks and cook for another 5 minutes until golden brown and crispy.
7. Serve immediately with syrup, powdered sugar, or your favorite dipping sauce.

Cooking Tips:

- Soak the bread sticks for a shorter time if you prefer them less eggy.
- For a crunchier texture, increase the cooking time by 1-2 minutes.

Air Fryer Doughnuts

Prep: 15 mins | Cook: 5 mins | Serves 6

Ingredients:

- 1 can of refrigerated biscuit dough
- 1/4 cup granulated sugar
- 1 teaspoon ground cinnamon
- 4 tablespoons melted butter

Instructions:

1. Preheat the air fryer to 350°F (177°C).
2. Separate the biscuits and use a small round cutter to remove the center of each biscuit to form doughnuts.
3. Mix the sugar and cinnamon in a shallow bowl and set aside.
4. Brush each doughnut with melted butter on both sides.
5. Place the doughnuts in the air fryer basket in a single layer, ensuring they do not touch.
6. Cook for 4 minutes, then flip and cook for an additional 1 minute or until golden brown.
7. Immediately toss the hot doughnuts in the cinnamon-sugar mixture to coat.
8. Serve warm.

Cooking Tips:

- Use the doughnut holes as well. Cook them for 3 minutes, flipping halfway.
- For glazed doughnuts, skip the cinnamon-sugar and drizzle with a mixture of powdered sugar and milk after they have cooled slightly.

Crispy Air Fryer Bacon

Prep: 2 mins | Cook: 10 mins | Serves 4

Ingredients:

- 8 slices of thick-cut bacon

Instructions:

1. Preheat the air fryer to 390°F (198°C).
2. Place the bacon slices in the air fryer basket in a single layer.
3. Cook for 10 minutes, flipping halfway through, or until the bacon reaches your desired level of crispness.
4. Transfer the bacon to a paper towel-lined plate to drain excess grease.

Cooking Tips:

- If cooking more than one layer of bacon, add a minute or two to the cooking time.
- For added flavor, sprinkle a little brown sugar on the bacon before cooking.

Air Fryer Hash Browns

Prep: 5 mins | Cook: 15 mins | Serves 2

Ingredients:

- 2 medium russet potatoes, peeled and grated
- 1 tablespoon olive oil
- Salt and pepper to taste

Instructions:

1. Preheat the air fryer to 400°F (204°C).
2. Squeeze out as much moisture as possible from the grated potatoes using a clean kitchen towel.
3. Toss the dried potatoes with olive oil, salt, and pepper in a bowl.
4. Form the mixture into patties and place them in the air fryer basket.
5. Cook for 15 minutes, flipping halfway through, until the hash browns are golden brown and crispy.
6. Serve hot with your favorite breakfast sides.

Cooking Tips:

- For extra flavor, mix in some shredded cheese or chopped herbs before cooking.
- Ensure the potatoes are dry to achieve maximum crispiness.

Air Fryer Sweet Potato Hash

Prep: 15 mins | Cook: 20 mins | Serves 4

Ingredients:

- 2 medium sweet potatoes, peeled and diced
- 1 red bell pepper, diced
- 1 green bell pepper, diced
- 1 medium onion, diced
- 2 tablespoons olive oil
- 1/2 teaspoon smoked paprika
- 1/2 teaspoon garlic powder
- Salt and pepper to taste
- 4 eggs (optional)

Instructions:

1. In a large bowl, toss the sweet potatoes, bell peppers, and onion with olive oil, smoked paprika, garlic powder, salt, and pepper.
2. Preheat the air fryer to 380°F (193°C).
3. Transfer the mixture to the air fryer basket and spread it out evenly.
4. Cook for 10 minutes, then stir the hash to ensure even cooking.
5. Continue to cook for another 8-10 minutes until the sweet potatoes are tender and slightly crispy.
6. If adding eggs, create four wells in the cooked hash and crack an egg into each well. Cook for an additional 3-4 minutes or until the eggs are cooked to your desired doneness.
7. Serve hot as a hearty breakfast or brunch dish.

Cooking Tips:

- Keep the sweet potato pieces small and uniform for even cooking.
- Top with fresh herbs like parsley or cilantro for an added flavor boost.

Breakfast Frittata in the Air Fryer

Prep: 10 mins | Cook: 20 mins | Serves 4

Ingredients:

- 6 eggs
- 1/4 cup milk
- 1/2 cup shredded cheese (your choice)
- 1/2 cup diced ham
- 1/2 cup chopped spinach
- Salt and pepper to taste
- Non-stick cooking spray

Instructions:

1. In a medium bowl, whisk together the eggs, milk, salt, and pepper.
2. Stir in the shredded cheese, diced ham, and chopped spinach.
3. Preheat the air fryer to 360°F (182°C).
4. Grease a baking pan that fits in your air fryer with non-stick cooking spray.
5. Pour the egg mixture into the prepared pan.
6. Place the pan in the air fryer basket and cook for 15-20 minutes, or until the frittata is set and lightly golden on top.
7. Let it cool for a few minutes before slicing and serving.

Cooking Tips:

- You can substitute any of your favorite vegetables or meats in this frittata.
- Let the frittata sit for a few minutes after cooking to make it easier to slice.

Air Fryer Apple Fritters

Prep: 15 mins | Cook: 10 mins | Serves 4

Ingredients:

- 1 cup all-purpose flour
- 1/4 cup granulated sugar
- 1 teaspoon baking powder
- 1/2 teaspoon ground cinnamon
- 1/4 teaspoon salt
- 1/3 cup milk
- 1 egg
- 1 teaspoon vanilla extract
- 1 cup finely chopped apples
- Powdered sugar for dusting

Instructions:

1. In a large bowl, combine flour, sugar, baking powder, cinnamon, and salt.
2. In another bowl, whisk together the milk, egg, and vanilla extract.
3. Pour the wet ingredients into the dry ingredients and stir until just combined.
4. Fold in the chopped apples.
5. Preheat the air fryer to 350°F (177°C).
6. Drop spoonfuls of the batter into the air fryer basket, making sure they are not touching.
7. Cook for 5 minutes, flip the fritters, and cook for an additional 5 minutes until golden brown and cooked through.
8. Dust with powdered sugar before serving.

Cooking Tips:

- For best results, use a tart apple variety like Granny Smith.
- Don't overcrowd the air fryer basket; cook in batches if necessary.

Air Fryer Sausage Breakfast Burritos

Prep: 15 mins | Cook: 12 mins | Serves 4

Ingredients:

- 4 large flour tortillas
- 8 sausage links, cooked and chopped
- 6 eggs, beaten
- 1/2 cup shredded cheddar cheese
- 1/4 cup diced bell pepper
- Salt and pepper to taste
- Salsa for serving

Instructions:

1. In a bowl, mix the beaten eggs with salt, pepper, and diced bell pepper.
2. Cook the egg mixture in a non-stick skillet over medium heat until scrambled and set aside.
3. Lay out the tortillas and evenly distribute the scrambled eggs, cooked sausage, and shredded cheese among them.
4. Roll up the burritos, tucking in the ends.
5. Preheat the air fryer to 380°F (193°C).
6. Place the burritos in the air fryer basket, seam side down, and cook for 6 minutes, then flip and cook for an additional 6 minutes until the tortillas are golden brown and crispy.
7. Serve with salsa on the side.

Cooking Tips:

- Wrap the burritos tightly to prevent filling from falling out during cooking.
- For a vegetarian version, replace the sausage with additional veggies or a meat substitute.

Air Fryer Breakfast Potatoes

Prep: 10 mins | Cook: 20 mins | Serves 4

Ingredients:

- 3 medium russet potatoes, diced
- 1 tablespoon olive oil
- 1 teaspoon garlic powder
- 1 teaspoon paprika
- Salt and pepper to taste
- 1/2 medium onion, diced
- 1/4 cup red bell pepper, diced

Instructions:

1. In a bowl, toss the diced potatoes with olive oil, garlic powder, paprika, salt, and pepper.
2. Preheat the air fryer to 400°F (204°C).
3. Add the potatoes to the air fryer basket and cook for 10 minutes.
4. Add the diced onion and bell pepper to the basket with the potatoes and cook for another 10 minutes, stirring halfway through, until the potatoes are crispy and the vegetables are tender.
5. Serve hot as a delicious side to any breakfast main course.

Cooking Tips:

- For extra flavor, toss the potatoes with fresh herbs like rosemary or thyme before cooking.
- Make sure the potatoes are cut into even-sized pieces for uniform cooking.

Air Fryer Egg Rolls

Prep: 20 mins | Cook: 10 mins | Serves 4

Ingredients:

- 8 egg roll wrappers
- 1 cup cooked and shredded chicken or pork (optional)
- 1 cup cabbage, shredded
- 1/2 cup carrots, shredded
- 1/4 cup green onions, sliced
- 2 tablespoons soy sauce
- 1 teaspoon ginger, grated
- 1 garlic clove, minced
- Olive oil spray

Instructions:

1. In a bowl, combine the chicken or pork (if using), cabbage, carrots, green onions, soy sauce, ginger, and garlic.
2. Place an egg roll wrapper on a flat surface and spoon approximately 2 tablespoons of the mixture into the center.
3. Fold the bottom corner over the filling, then fold in the sides and roll tightly. Seal the final corner with a little water.
4. Preheat the air fryer to 390°F (199°C).
5. Spray the air fryer basket with olive oil spray and place the egg rolls in the basket. Spray the tops of the egg rolls with more olive oil.
6. Cook for 5 minutes, turn the egg rolls, and cook for another 5 minutes until they are golden brown and crispy.
7. Serve hot with dipping sauce of choice.

Cooking Tips:

- Do not overcrowd the basket; cook in batches if necessary for the best texture.
- For a vegetarian option, omit the meat and add more vegetables or tofu.

Air Fryer Breakfast Pizza

Prep: 5 mins | Cook: 8 mins | Serves 2

Ingredients:

- 2 pre-made individual-sized pizza crusts
- 1/2 cup pizza sauce
- 1 cup mozzarella cheese, shredded
- 4 breakfast sausage links, cooked and sliced
- 1/2 cup bell pepper, diced
- 4 eggs, beaten
- Salt and pepper to taste

Instructions:

1. Preheat the air fryer to 360°F (182°C).
2. Spread pizza sauce on each crust, leaving a small border around the edges.
3. Sprinkle shredded mozzarella cheese over the sauce.
4. Top with slices of breakfast sausage and diced bell pepper.
5. Carefully pour the beaten eggs over the toppings, trying to keep the eggs on top.
6. Season with salt and pepper.
7. Place the pizzas in the air fryer basket and cook for 8 minutes or until the eggs are set and the cheese is melted and bubbly.
8. Slice and serve immediately.

Cooking Tips:

- For a crispier crust, pre-cook the crusts for 2-3 minutes before adding toppings.
- Customize your breakfast pizza with additional toppings like onions, mushrooms, or bacon.

Air Fryer Blueberry Muffins

Prep: 10 mins | Cook: 15 mins | Serves 6

Ingredients:

- 1 1/2 cups all-purpose flour
- 3/4 cup granulated sugar
- 1/2 teaspoon salt
- 2 teaspoons baking powder
- 1/3 cup vegetable oil
- 1 egg
- 1/3 cup milk
- 1 cup fresh blueberries

Instructions:

1. In a mixing bowl, combine flour, sugar, salt, and baking powder.
2. Add in vegetable oil, egg, and milk and mix until just combined.
3. Gently fold in the blueberries.
4. Preheat the air fryer to 320°F (160°C).
5. Fill silicone muffin cups about two-thirds full with the batter and place them in the air fryer basket.
6. Cook for 15 minutes or until a toothpick inserted into the center of a muffin comes out clean.
7. Allow to cool slightly before serving.

Cooking Tips:

- Do not overmix the batter to ensure the muffins remain tender.
- If using frozen blueberries, do not thaw them before adding to the batter to prevent discoloration.

Air Fryer Cinnamon and Sugar Doughnuts

Prep: 15 mins | Cook: 10 mins | Serves 6

Ingredients:

- 1 can refrigerated biscuit dough
- 1/4 cup melted butter
- 1/2 cup granulated sugar
- 1 tablespoon ground cinnamon

Instructions:

1. Cut a hole in the center of each biscuit to shape the doughnuts.
2. Preheat the air fryer to 360°F (182°C).
3. Place doughnuts in the air fryer basket, making sure they are not touching, and cook for 5 minutes.
4. Flip the doughnuts and cook for an additional 5 minutes until golden brown.
5. Meanwhile, mix the sugar and cinnamon in a shallow dish.
6. Brush the warm doughnuts with melted butter and then dip them into the cinnamon-sugar mixture to coat.
7. Serve warm for best flavor.

Cooking Tips:

- For extra flavor, add a pinch of nutmeg to the cinnamon-sugar mixture.
- Use a small round cutter to make uniform holes in the doughnuts.

Air Fryer Breakfast Bombs

Prep: 20 mins | Cook: 10 mins | Serves 4

Ingredients:

- 8 slices of bread, crusts removed
- 4 eggs, scrambled
- 8 slices of bacon, cooked and crumbled
- 1 cup shredded cheddar cheese
- 2 tablespoons milk
- Salt and pepper to taste

Instructions:

1. Flatten each slice of bread with a rolling pin.
2. In a bowl, mix the scrambled eggs, cooked bacon crumbles, shredded cheese, milk, salt, and pepper.
3. Place a spoonful of the egg mixture in the center of each flattened bread slice.
4. Pull the corners of the bread up and around the filling, then pinch to seal, forming a ball.
5. Preheat the air fryer to 380°F (193°C).
6. Place the breakfast bombs in the air fryer basket and cook for 10 minutes, or until the bread is golden brown and crispy.
7. Serve hot with a side of salsa or hot sauce.

Cooking Tips:

- Add a small slice of avocado or a dollop of cream cheese to the egg mixture for added creaminess.
- Ensure the edges of the bread are sealed well to prevent the filling from leaking out during cooking.

Air Fryer Breakfast Casserole

Prep: 15 mins | Cook: 20 mins | Serves 4

Ingredients:

- 6 large eggs
- 1/2 cup milk
- 1 cup shredded cheddar cheese
- 1/2 cup diced ham
- 1/2 cup bell pepper, chopped
- 1/2 cup onion, chopped
- Salt and pepper to taste
- Non-stick cooking spray

Instructions:

1. In a large bowl, whisk together eggs and milk. Season with salt and pepper.
2. Stir in the cheddar cheese, diced ham, bell pepper, and onion.
3. Spray a suitable ovenproof dish that fits into the air fryer basket with non-stick cooking spray.
4. Pour the egg mixture into the prepared dish.
5. Preheat the air fryer to 320°F (160°C).
6. Place the dish in the air fryer basket and cook for 20 minutes, or until the eggs are set and the top is golden brown.
7. Let the casserole sit for a few minutes before slicing. Serve warm.

Cooking Tips:

- You can substitute the ham for sausage, bacon, or a vegetarian protein option.
- Feel free to add vegetables such as spinach or mushrooms for extra nutrients and flavor.

Air Fryer Banana Bread

Prep: 10 mins | Cook: 40 mins | Serves 6

Ingredients:

- 2 ripe bananas, mashed
- 1/3 cup melted butter
- 1/2 cup sugar
- 1 egg, beaten
- 1 teaspoon vanilla extract
- 1 teaspoon baking soda
- Pinch of salt
- 1 1/2 cups of all-purpose flour

Instructions:

1. In a mixing bowl, combine mashed bananas and melted butter.
2. Mix in sugar, egg, and vanilla.
3. Sprinkle the baking soda and salt over the mixture and blend in.
4. Add the flour and mix until it is just incorporated.
5. Pour the batter into a greased and floured pan that fits in your air fryer.
6. Preheat the air fryer to 330°F (165°C).
7. Bake for 40 minutes or until a toothpick inserted into the center comes out clean.
8. Let the banana bread cool before slicing.

Cooking Tips:

Ensure the pan is not too tall for your air fryer there should be enough space for air circulation.
If the bread starts to brown too much, cover it with foil for the remainder of the cooking time.

Air Fryer Breakfast Poppers

Prep: 10 mins | Cook: 10 mins | Serves 4

Ingredients:

- 1 cup breakfast sausage, cooked and crumbled
- 1 cup tater tots, thawed and chopped
- 1/2 cup shredded cheddar cheese
- 4 large eggs
- Salt and pepper to taste
- Non-stick cooking spray

Instructions:

1. In a bowl, mix together the sausage, tater tots, and cheddar cheese.
2. Crack the eggs into the mixture, season with salt and pepper, and stir to combine.
3. Spray a mini muffin tin that will fit into your air fryer with non-stick cooking spray.
4. Spoon the mixture into the muffin cups.
5. Preheat the air fryer to 350°F (177°C).
6. Place the muffin tin in the air fryer basket and cook for 10 minutes, or until the eggs are set.
7. Carefully remove the breakfast poppers and let them cool slightly before serving.

Cooking Tips:

- For a lighter version, use turkey sausage and low-fat cheese.
- Serve with a dollop of sour cream or salsa for added flavor.

Air Fryer Omelette Bites

Prep: 10 mins | Cook: 8 mins | Serves 4

Ingredients:

- 6 large eggs
- 1/4 cup milk
- 1/2 cup diced vegetables (peppers, onions, mushrooms)
- 1/2 cup shredded cheese
- Salt and pepper to taste
- Non-stick cooking spray

Instructions:

1. In a bowl, whisk together the eggs and milk. Season with salt and pepper.
2. Stir in the diced vegetables and shredded cheese.
3. Spray a silicone muffin pan with non-stick cooking spray and fill each cup with the egg mixture.
4. Preheat the air fryer to 300°F (149°C).
5. Cook the omelette bites for 8 minutes, or until they are firm and cooked through.
6. Remove from the air fryer and let cool for a minute before removing from the muffin cups.

Cooking Tips:

- Avoid overfilling the muffin cups to prevent the eggs from spilling over.
- These omelette bites can be customized with various fillings such as ham, bacon, or spinach.

Air Fryer Baked Oatmeal

Prep: 5 mins | Cook: 15 mins | Serves 2

Ingredients:

- 1 cup rolled oats
- 1 banana, mashed
- 1/4 cup milk
- 1 tablespoon honey or maple syrup
- 1/2 teaspoon cinnamon
- 1/4 cup mix-ins (nuts, berries, chocolate chips)
- Non-stick cooking spray

Instructions:

1. In a bowl, combine the oats, mashed banana, milk, honey, and cinnamon.
2. Stir in your choice of mix-ins.
3. Spray two small baking dishes that fit in your air fryer with non-stick cooking spray.
4. Divide the oatmeal mixture between the dishes.
5. Preheat the air fryer to 350°F (177°C).
6. Cook for 15 minutes, or until the top is set and slightly golden.
7. Serve warm with additional toppings like yogurt or fruit if desired.

Cooking Tips:

- If you prefer a softer texture, add an extra tablespoon or two of milk before cooking.
- For a vegan version, use a plant-based milk and substitute honey with maple syrup.

Chapter 2: Main Dishes

Cajun Air Fryer Salmon

Prep: 5 mins | Cook: 10 mins | Serves 2

Ingredients:

- 2 salmon fillets (about 6 ounces each)
- 1 tablespoon olive oil
- 1 tablespoon Cajun seasoning
- Lemon wedges, for serving

Instructions:

1. Rub each salmon fillet with olive oil and then coat generously with Cajun seasoning.
2. Preheat the air fryer to 400°F (200°C).
3. Place the salmon fillets in the air fryer basket, skin-side down.
4. Cook for 10 minutes, or until the salmon is cooked through and flakes easily with a fork.
5. Serve hot with lemon wedges on the side.

Cooking Tips:

- Adjust the cooking time depending on the thickness of the salmon fillets.
- If you prefer a less spicy flavor, reduce the amount of Cajun seasoning.

Mexican-Style Air Fryer Stuffed Chicken Breasts

Prep: 15 mins | Cook: 22 mins | Serves 4

Ingredients:

- 4 boneless, skinless chicken breasts
- 1/2 cup cream cheese, softened
- 1/2 cup shredded Mexican cheese blend
- 1/4 cup diced green chilies
- 1/4 cup chopped fresh cilantro
- 1 teaspoon chili powder
- 1 teaspoon garlic powder
- Salt and pepper to taste
- 1 tablespoon olive oil

Instructions:

1. In a bowl, mix together cream cheese, Mexican cheese blend, green chilies, cilantro, chili powder, and garlic powder. Season with salt and pepper.
2. Cut a pocket into the side of each chicken breast.
3. Stuff the cheese mixture into each pocket and secure with toothpicks.
4. Brush each chicken breast with olive oil and season the outside with salt and pepper.
5. Preheat the air fryer to 370°F (188°C).
6. Cook the chicken breasts in the air fryer for 22 minutes, or until the chicken is cooked through and the juices run clear.
7. Let rest for a few minutes before serving.

Cooking Tips:

- Make sure to not overfill the chicken breasts, as the filling can ooze out during cooking.
- You can also wrap the stuffed breasts in bacon for extra flavor and crispiness.

Air Fryer Herb-Crusted Salmon with Potatoes

Prep: 10 mins | Cook: 20 mins | Serves 2

Ingredients:

- 2 salmon fillets (about 6 ounces each)
- 1 pound baby potatoes, halved
- 2 tablespoons olive oil
- 2 teaspoons dried Italian herbs
- Salt and pepper to taste
- Lemon wedges, for serving

Instructions:

1. Toss the baby potatoes with 1 tablespoon olive oil, 1 teaspoon Italian herbs, salt, and pepper.
2. Preheat the air fryer to 400°F (200°C).
3. Place the potatoes in the air fryer basket and cook for 10 minutes.
4. Meanwhile, brush the salmon with the remaining olive oil and season with the remaining Italian herbs, salt, and pepper.
5. After the potatoes have cooked for 10 minutes, stir them and add the salmon fillets to the basket.
6. Cook for an additional 10 minutes, or until the salmon is cooked through and the potatoes are tender.
7. Serve hot with lemon wedges on the side.

Cooking Tips:

- Make sure the potatoes are cut into even-sized pieces for even cooking.
- If your air fryer is small, cook the potatoes and salmon in batches to avoid overcrowding.

Air Fryer Burrito-Stuffed Chicken

Prep: 20 mins | Cook: 20 mins | Serves 4

Ingredients:

- 4 boneless, skinless chicken breasts
- 1 cup cooked rice
- 1/2 cup canned black beans, drained and rinsed
- 1/2 cup corn kernels
- 1/2 cup shredded cheddar cheese
- 1 teaspoon ground cumin
- 1 teaspoon paprika
- Salt and pepper to taste
- 1 tablespoon olive oil
- Salsa and sour cream, for serving

Instructions:

1. In a bowl, combine cooked rice, black beans, corn, cheddar cheese, cumin, paprika, salt, and pepper.
2. Cut a pocket into the side of each chicken breast and stuff with the rice mixture.
3. Secure the openings with toothpicks.
4. Brush each chicken breast with olive oil and season with additional salt and pepper.
5. Preheat the air fryer to 370°F (188°C).
6. Cook the chicken breasts for 20 minutes, or until the chicken is cooked through.
7. Serve with salsa and sour cream on the side.

Cooking Tips:

- Be careful not to overstuff the chicken, as the filling can spill out during the cooking process.
- For an extra kick, add chopped jalapeños or chili flakes to the rice mixture.

Air Fryer Baby Back Ribs

Prep: 10 mins | Cook: 25 mins | Serves 2-3

Ingredients:

- 1 rack baby back ribs (about 2 pounds)
- 2 tablespoons barbecue rub
- 1/2 cup barbecue sauce

Instructions:

1. Season the baby back ribs all over with the barbecue rub.
2. Cut the rack into sections that will fit into your air fryer basket.
3. Preheat the air fryer to 360°F (182°C).
4. Place the rib sections in the air fryer basket and cook for 25 minutes, flipping halfway through.
5. In the last 5 minutes of cooking, brush the ribs with barbecue sauce.
6. Serve hot with extra barbecue sauce on the side.

Cooking Tips:

- Let the ribs rest for a few minutes after cooking for the juices to redistribute.
- For fall-off-the-bone tenderness, you can wrap the ribs in foil and cook for an additional 5 minutes.

Air Fryer Meatloaf

Prep: 10 mins | Cook: 40 mins | Serves 4

Ingredients:

- 1 pound ground beef
- 1/4 cup breadcrumbs
- 1 egg
- 1/4 cup milk
- 1/4 cup diced onion
- 2 cloves garlic, minced
- 1 tablespoon Worcestershire sauce
- 1 teaspoon salt
- 1/2 teaspoon black pepper
- 1/2 cup ketchup (for glazing)

Instructions:

1. In a large bowl, combine the ground beef, breadcrumbs, egg, milk, onion, garlic, Worcestershire sauce, salt, and pepper. Mix until just combined.
2. Form the mixture into a loaf shape that will fit in your air fryer basket.
3. Preheat the air fryer to 370°F (188°C).
4. Place the meatloaf in the air fryer and cook for 30 minutes.
5. Glaze the meatloaf with ketchup and continue to cook for an additional 10 minutes, or until the meatloaf reaches an internal temperature of 160°F (71°C).
6. Let the meatloaf rest for 5 minutes before slicing.

Cooking Tips:

- Avoid overmixing the meat to keep the meatloaf tender.
- Placing a piece of parchment paper beneath the meatloaf can make removal easier and aid in cleanup.

Air Fryer Mac and Cheese

Prep: 5 mins | Cook: 15 mins | Serves 4

Ingredients:

- 2 cups cooked macaroni
- 1 cup shredded cheddar cheese
- 1/2 cup whole milk
- 2 tablespoons butter
- 1/4 teaspoon paprika
- Salt and pepper to taste
- Bread crumbs for topping (optional)

Instructions:

1. In a bowl, combine the cooked macaroni, cheddar cheese, milk, butter, paprika, salt, and pepper.
2. Transfer the mixture into a baking dish that fits in your air fryer.
3. Sprinkle bread crumbs on top if using.
4. Preheat the air fryer to 360°F (182°C).
5. Cook for 15 minutes, or until the cheese is melted and bubbly.
6. Serve hot.

Cooking Tips:

- If you prefer a crispier topping, you can mix the breadcrumbs with melted butter before sprinkling them over the mac and cheese.
- Stir the mac and cheese halfway through cooking for even melting.

Air Fryer Lobster Tails

Prep: 5 mins | Cook: 8 mins | Serves 2

Ingredients:

- 2 lobster tails
- 2 tablespoons melted butter
- 1 teaspoon paprika
- Salt and pepper to taste
- Lemon wedges, for serving

Instructions:

1. Using kitchen shears, cut a lengthwise slit down the center of the lobster tails' shell.
2. Gently pry the shell open and lift the lobster meat to rest on top of the shell.
3. Brush the lobster meat with melted butter and season with paprika, salt, and pepper.
4. Preheat the air fryer to 380°F (193°C).
5. Place the lobster tails in the air fryer and cook for 8 minutes, or until the meat is opaque and cooked through.
6. Serve immediately with lemon wedges.

Cooking Tips:

- Be careful not to overcook the lobster, as it can become tough. Start checking for doneness after about 5 minutes.
- For extra flavor, you can add minced garlic to the melted butter.

Air Fryer Steak

Prep: 5 mins | Cook: 12 mins | Serves 2

Ingredients:

- 2 steaks (ribeye, sirloin, or your choice), about 1-inch thick
- 1 tablespoon olive oil
- Salt and pepper to taste

Instructions:

1. Brush each steak with olive oil and generously season with salt and pepper.
2. Let the steaks sit at room temperature for about 20 minutes before cooking.
3. Preheat the air fryer to 400°F (200°C).
4. Place the steaks in the air fryer basket and cook for about 12 minutes for medium-rare (or longer for your preferred doneness), flipping halfway through.
5. Let the steaks rest for 5 minutes before slicing and serving.

Cooking Tips:

- The cook time will vary depending on the thickness of the steak and your preferred level of doneness.
- Allow the steak to rest after cooking to ensure the juices redistribute for a moist and tender result.

Air Fryer Corn on the Cob

Prep: 2 mins | Cook: 10 mins | Serves 4

Ingredients:

- 4 ears of corn, husked and cleaned
- 1 tablespoon olive oil
- Salt and pepper to taste
- Butter, for serving

Instructions:

1. Brush each ear of corn with olive oil and season with salt and pepper.
2. Preheat the air fryer to 380°F (193°C).
3. Place the corn in the air fryer basket and cook for 10 minutes, turning halfway through the cooking time.
4. Serve hot with butter.

Cooking Tips:

- For extra flavor, sprinkle your favorite seasonings like chili powder, garlic powder, or herbs over the corn before cooking.
- If the corn is particularly large, you may need to cook it in batches to avoid overcrowding.

Air Fryer Pasta Tacos

Prep: 15 mins | Cook: 10 mins | Serves 4

Ingredients:

- 8 oz pasta shells, cooked and drained
- 1 cup marinara sauce
- 1 cup shredded mozzarella cheese
- 1/2 cup grated Parmesan cheese
- 1 tablespoon Italian seasoning
- 12 small corn tortillas
- Cooking spray
- Optional toppings: sour cream, chopped cilantro, diced tomatoes

Instructions:

1. In a bowl, mix the cooked pasta with marinara sauce, mozzarella, Parmesan, and Italian seasoning.
2. Warm the tortillas slightly to prevent breaking when folding. Place a spoonful of the pasta mixture into the center of each tortilla, fold gently.
3. Preheat the air fryer to 380°F (193°C). Spray the air fryer basket with cooking spray.
4. Place the tacos in the air fryer in a single layer, spraying the tops with cooking spray. You may need to work in batches.
5. Air fry for 5 minutes until the tortillas are crispy and the filling is heated through.
6. Serve with optional toppings as desired.

Cooking Tips:

- Ensure the pasta is not overcooked as it will cook further in the air fryer.
- To add a crisp to your taco shells, spray them lightly with oil before air frying.

Air Fryer Pork Chops

Prep: 5 mins | Cook: 12 mins | Serves 4

Ingredients:

- 4 boneless pork chops, about 1-inch thick
- 1 teaspoon garlic powder
- 1 teaspoon smoked paprika
- Salt and pepper to taste
- Olive oil spray

Instructions:

1. Season the pork chops with garlic powder, smoked paprika, salt, and pepper.
2. Spray each pork chop lightly with olive oil.
3. Preheat the air fryer to 400°F (200°C).
4. Cook the pork chops for 12 minutes, flipping halfway through, or until the internal temperature reaches 145°F (63°C).
5. Allow the chops to rest for 5 minutes before serving.

Cooking Tips:

- For added flavor, marinate the pork chops for at least 30 minutes before cooking.
- Use an instant-read thermometer to avoid overcooking.

Air Fryer Chicken Parmesan

Prep: 10 mins | Cook: 12 mins | Serves 4

Ingredients:

- 4 boneless, skinless chicken breasts
- 1/2 cup all-purpose flour
- 2 large eggs, beaten
- 1 cup Italian breadcrumbs
- 1/2 cup grated Parmesan cheese
- 1 cup marinara sauce
- 1 cup shredded mozzarella cheese
- Salt and pepper to taste
- Olive oil spray

Instructions:

1. Season the chicken breasts with salt and pepper. Dredge in flour, dip into beaten eggs, then coat in a mixture of breadcrumbs and Parmesan.
2. Preheat the air fryer to 360°F (182°C). Spray the air fryer basket with olive oil.
3. Place the chicken in the basket and spray the tops with olive oil. Cook for 6 minutes.
4. Flip the chicken, top with marinara and mozzarella. Cook for another 6 minutes, or until chicken is cooked through and cheese is melted.
5. Serve with pasta and extra marinara if desired.

Cooking Tips:

- Ensure the chicken is an even thickness for uniform cooking.
- Spray the breaded chicken with oil to help achieve a golden-brown crust.

Goat Cheese Stuffed Chicken

Prep: 15 mins | Cook: 22 mins | Serves 4

Ingredients:

- 4 chicken breasts
- 4 oz goat cheese
- 2 tablespoons chopped spinach
- Salt and pepper to taste
- 1 teaspoon garlic powder
- Olive oil spray

Instructions:

1. Make a horizontal cut in the side of each chicken breast to create a pocket. Be careful not to cut all the way through.
2. Mix goat cheese and spinach. Season the mixture with salt and pepper.
3. Stuff each chicken breast with the goat cheese mixture. Secure with toothpicks if needed.
4. Season the outside of the chicken with garlic powder, salt, and pepper.
5. Spray each chicken breast with olive oil.
6. Preheat the air fryer to 370°F (188°C).
7. Cook the stuffed chicken breasts for 22 minutes, flipping halfway through, or until the internal temperature reaches 165°F (74°C).
8. Let rest for 5 minutes before serving.

Cooking Tips:

- Don't overfill the pockets to prevent the filling from leaking out.
- Let the chicken rest to allow the cheese to set slightly, making it easier to cut.

Air Fryer Hot Pockets

Prep: 20 mins | Cook: 15 mins | Serves 4

Ingredients:

- 1 package refrigerated pizza dough
- 1 cup of your preferred filling (e.g., ham and cheese, pepperoni and marinara, vegetables and cheese)
- 1 beaten egg for egg wash
- Olive oil spray

Instructions:

1. Roll out the pizza dough and cut into 8 equal-sized rectangles.
2. Place a spoonful of filling on one side of each rectangle, leaving room at the edges to seal.
3. Fold the dough over the filling to create a pocket. Press the edges with a fork to seal.
4. Brush the tops with egg wash and lightly spray with olive oil.
5. Preheat the air fryer to 350°F (177°C).
6. Place the pockets in the air fryer basket, ensuring they do not touch. Cook for 15 minutes, until golden brown.
7. Serve warm with a side of marinara sauce for dipping, if desired.

Cooking Tips:

- Don't overfill the pockets to prevent the filling from spilling out during cooking.
- If the edges aren't sealing, you can dab a small amount of water on them before pressing with a fork.

Air Fryer Gochujang Chicken Wings

Prep: 10 mins | Cook: 24 mins | Serves 4

Ingredients:

- 2 lbs chicken wings, tips removed, drumettes and flats separated
- 1 tablespoon baking powder
- 1/2 cup Gochujang (Korean chili paste)
- 2 tablespoons honey
- 1 tablespoon soy sauce
- 1 tablespoon rice vinegar
- 1 teaspoon sesame oil
- Sesame seeds and sliced green onions for garnish

Instructions:

1. Pat the chicken wings dry with paper towels. Toss with baking powder and a pinch of salt.
2. Preheat the air fryer to 380°F (193°C).
3. Arrange the wings in a single layer in the air fryer basket. Cook for 24 minutes, flipping halfway through.
4. While the wings cook, whisk together Gochujang, honey, soy sauce, rice vinegar, and sesame oil in a bowl.
5. Once the wings are done, toss them in the sauce until well coated.
6. Garnish with sesame seeds and green onions before serving.

Cooking Tips:

- Make sure the wings are dry before tossing with baking powder for extra crispiness.
- Let the wings rest for 5 minutes after cooking so the sauce can adhere better.

Air Fryer Shrimp Scampi

Prep: 5 mins | Cook: 8 mins | Serves 4

Ingredients:

- 1 lb large shrimp, peeled and deveined
- 3 tablespoons unsalted butter, melted
- 4 cloves garlic, minced
- 1 tablespoon lemon juice
- 2 tablespoons chopped parsley
- Salt and pepper to taste
- Lemon wedges for serving

Instructions:

1. Toss the shrimp with melted butter, garlic, lemon juice, parsley, salt, and pepper.
2. Preheat the air fryer to 370°F (188°C).
3. Place the shrimp in the air fryer basket in a single layer. Cook for 8 minutes, shaking the basket halfway through.
4. Serve with additional lemon wedges on the side.

Cooking Tips:

- Don't overcrowd the basket; cook in batches if necessary for even cooking.
- Keep an eye on the shrimp as they can quickly become overcooked.

Air Fryer Indonesian-Style Chicken Wings

Prep: 15 mins | Cook: 24 mins | Serves 4

Ingredients:

- 2 lbs chicken wings, tips removed, drumettes and flats separated
- 1/4 cup soy sauce
- 2 tablespoons Indonesian sweet soy sauce (kecap manis)
- 1 tablespoon honey
- 1 tablespoon lime juice
- 1 teaspoon grated ginger
- 1 garlic clove, minced
- Crushed peanuts and sliced green onions for garnish

Instructions:

1. In a large bowl, combine soy sauce, sweet soy sauce, honey, lime juice, ginger, and garlic. Marinate the chicken wings for at least 30 minutes.
2. Preheat the air fryer to 380°F (193°C).
3. Remove wings from marinade and arrange in the air fryer basket in a single layer. Reserve the marinade for basting.
4. Cook for 24 minutes, flipping and basting with the marinade every 8 minutes.
5. Garnish with crushed peanuts and green onions before serving.

Cooking Tips:

- Marinating the wings longer (up to overnight) will intensify the flavors.
- Basting the wings during cooking will help develop a flavorful glaze.

Air Fryer Crispy Tofu with Asian Glaze

Prep: 10 mins | Cook: 15 mins | Serves 4

Ingredients:

- 1 block (14 oz) extra-firm tofu, pressed and cubed
- 1 tablespoon cornstarch
- 2 tablespoons soy sauce
- 1 tablespoon hoisin sauce
- 1 tablespoon honey or maple syrup
- 1 teaspoon sesame oil
- 1 garlic clove, minced
- 1 teaspoon grated ginger
- Sesame seeds and sliced green onions for garnish

Instructions:

1. Toss the tofu cubes with cornstarch until evenly coated.
2. Preheat the air fryer to 400°F (200°C).
3. Arrange the tofu in the air fryer basket in a single layer. Cook for 15 minutes, shaking the basket occasionally, until crispy.
4. Meanwhile, combine soy sauce, hoisin sauce, honey, sesame oil, garlic, and ginger in a bowl to create the glaze.
5. Once the tofu is cooked, toss it in the glaze until well coated.
6. Garnish with sesame seeds and green onions before serving.

Cooking Tips:

- Pressing the tofu is key to getting it crispy; remove as much moisture as possible before cooking.
- The glaze can be thickened with a little cornstarch if desired.

Air Fryer Stuffed Peppers

Prep: 15 mins | Cook: 20 mins | Serves 4

Ingredients:

- 4 bell peppers, tops removed and seeded
- 1/2 lb ground beef or turkey
- 1/2 cup cooked rice
- 1/4 cup tomato sauce
- 1/4 cup shredded cheese
- 1/4 cup chopped onions
- 1 garlic clove, minced
- 1 teaspoon cumin
- Salt and pepper to taste

Instructions:

1. In a bowl, mix the ground meat, rice, tomato sauce, cheese, onions, garlic, cumin, salt, and pepper.
2. Stuff the mixture into the bell peppers.
3. Preheat the air fryer to 350°F (177°C).
4. Place the stuffed peppers in the air fryer basket. Cook for 20 minutes, or until the meat is cooked through and the peppers are tender.
5. Serve hot.

Cooking Tips:

- For vegetarian stuffed peppers, substitute meat with quinoa or additional vegetables.
- Adding a little water to the bottom of the air fryer basket can help to keep the peppers moist while cooking.

Chapter 3: Vegetables and Side Dishes

Air Fryer Broccoli Parmesan

Prep: 5 mins | Cook: 8 mins | Serves 4

Ingredients:

- 1 head of broccoli, cut into florets
- 2 tablespoons olive oil
- 1/4 cup grated Parmesan cheese
- 1/2 teaspoon garlic powder
- Salt and pepper to taste
- Lemon wedges for serving

Instructions:

1. In a bowl, toss broccoli florets with olive oil, garlic powder, salt, and pepper.
2. Preheat the air fryer to 375°F (190°C).
3. Place the broccoli in the air fryer basket in a single layer. Cook for 6 minutes.
4. Sprinkle Parmesan cheese over the broccoli and cook for an additional 2 minutes, until the cheese is melted and broccoli is tender.
5. Serve with lemon wedges on the side.

Cooking Tips:

- For extra flavor, add a pinch of red pepper flakes before cooking.
- Ensure the broccoli is in a single layer for even cooking; you may need to cook in batches.

Air Fryer Sweet Potato Fries

Prep: 10 mins | Cook: 15 mins | Serves 4

Ingredients:

- 2 large sweet potatoes, peeled and cut into 1/4-inch sticks
- 2 tablespoons olive oil
- 1 teaspoon paprika
- Salt and pepper to taste

Instructions:

1. Soak the sweet potato sticks in cold water for 30 minutes to remove excess starch.
2. Drain and pat dry the sweet potatoes, then toss with olive oil, paprika, salt, and pepper.
3. Preheat the air fryer to 380°F (193°C).
4. Arrange the sweet potato fries in the air fryer basket in a single layer. Cook for 15 minutes, shaking the basket halfway through.
5. Serve immediately for the best texture.

Cooking Tips:

- Soaking the sweet potatoes is a crucial step for crispy fries.
- Don't overcrowd the air fryer; cook in batches if needed.

Garlic Parmesan Air Fryer Carrot Fries

Prep: 10 mins | Cook: 14 mins | Serves 4

Ingredients:

- 6 large carrots, peeled and cut into 1/4-inch sticks
- 2 tablespoons olive oil
- 1/4 cup grated Parmesan cheese
- 1 teaspoon garlic powder
- Salt and pepper to taste

Instructions:

1. Toss the carrot sticks with olive oil, garlic powder, salt, and pepper.
2. Preheat the air fryer to 380°F (193°C).
3. Cook the carrots in the air fryer basket for 12 minutes.
4. Sprinkle Parmesan cheese over the carrots and cook for an additional 2 minutes, until the cheese is melted and carrots are tender.
5. Serve warm.

Cooking Tips:

- Ensure carrots are cut evenly for uniform cooking.
- For a dairy-free version, omit the Parmesan or use a vegan alternative.

Air-Fryer Garlic-Rosemary Brussels Sprouts

Prep: 10 mins | Cook: 12 mins | Serves 4

Ingredients:

- 1 lb Brussels sprouts, trimmed and halved
- 2 tablespoons olive oil
- 1 tablespoon minced garlic
- 1 teaspoon chopped fresh rosemary
- Salt and pepper to taste

Instructions:

1. Toss Brussels sprouts with olive oil, garlic, rosemary, salt, and pepper.
2. Preheat the air fryer to 380°F (193°C).
3. Place the Brussels sprouts in the air fryer basket in a single layer. Cook for 12 minutes, shaking the basket halfway through.
4. Serve hot.

Cooking Tips:

- For added crispiness, increase the cooking time by a few minutes.
- If you're using frozen Brussels sprouts, adjust cooking time accordingly and ensure they are thawed and well-drained before use.

Air Fryer Zucchini Chips

Prep: 10 mins | Cook: 10 mins | Serves 4

Ingredients:

- 2 medium zucchinis, thinly sliced
- 1 tablespoon olive oil
- 1/2 cup Panko breadcrumbs
- 1/4 cup grated Parmesan cheese
- 1 teaspoon Italian seasoning
- Salt and pepper to taste

Instructions:

1. Preheat the air fryer to 370°F (188°C).
2. In a bowl, toss zucchini slices with olive oil, salt, and pepper.
3. In another bowl, mix Panko, Parmesan, and Italian seasoning.
4. Dip zucchini slices in the breadcrumb mixture, pressing to adhere.
5. Arrange zucchini slices in the air fryer basket in a single layer; cook for 10 minutes, flipping halfway through.
6. Serve immediately.

Cooking Tips:

- Use a mandolin for evenly sliced zucchini.
- Serve with a dipping sauce like marinara or ranch for added flavor.

Italian-Style Air-Fried Ratatouille

Prep: 15 mins | Cook: 20 mins | Serves 4

Ingredients:

- 1 small eggplant, cut into 1/2-inch cubes
- 1 zucchini, cut into 1/2-inch slices
- 1 yellow squash, cut into 1/2-inch slices
- 1 bell pepper, cut into 1-inch pieces
- 1 small red onion, cut into wedges
- 2 tomatoes, chopped
- 3 tablespoons olive oil
- 2 garlic cloves, minced
- 1 teaspoon dried oregano
- 1 teaspoon dried basil
- Salt and pepper to taste
- Fresh basil leaves for garnish

Instructions:

1. In a large bowl, combine eggplant, zucchini, yellow squash, bell pepper, red onion, and tomatoes. Toss with olive oil, minced garlic, oregano, basil, salt, and pepper until well coated.
2. Preheat the air fryer to 380°F (193°C).
3. Transfer the vegetable mixture to the air fryer basket, and cook for 20 minutes, stirring halfway through, until vegetables are tender and lightly browned.
4. Garnish with fresh basil leaves before serving.

Cooking Tips:

- For best results, cut vegetables into uniform sizes for even cooking.
- Drizzle with balsamic glaze before serving for an extra flavor boost.

Rosemary Potato Wedges for Air Fryer

Prep: 10 mins | Cook: 18 mins | Serves 4

Ingredients:

- 4 medium potatoes, cut into wedges
- 2 tablespoons olive oil
- 1 tablespoon fresh rosemary, chopped
- Salt and pepper to taste

Instructions:

1. Soak potato wedges in cold water for at least 30 minutes to remove excess starch.
2. Drain and pat the potatoes dry, then toss with olive oil, rosemary, salt, and pepper.
3. Preheat the air fryer to 400°F (204°C).
4. Arrange potato wedges in the air fryer basket. Cook for 18 minutes, turning halfway through, until golden brown and crisp.
5. Serve immediately.

Cooking Tips:

- Soaking the potatoes is a key step for achieving a crispy texture.
- Sprinkle with Parmesan cheese after cooking for an additional flavor dimension.

Air Fryer Green Beans with Crispy Shallots

Prep: 10 mins | Cook: 12 mins | Serves 4

Ingredients:

- 1 lb green beans, trimmed
- 2 shallots, thinly sliced
- 1 tablespoon olive oil
- Salt and pepper to taste

Instructions:

1. Toss green beans and shallots with olive oil, salt, and pepper.
2. Preheat the air fryer to 370°F (188°C).
3. Place the green beans and shallots in the air fryer basket, and cook for 12 minutes, shaking the basket occasionally, until the beans are tender and shallots are crispy.
4. Serve immediately.

Cooking Tips:

- Ensure green beans are dry before tossing with oil for better crispness.
- Add a splash of lemon juice after cooking for a zesty finish.

Air Fryer Vegetables Medley with Garlic and Herbs

Prep: 10 mins | Cook: 15 mins | Serves 4

Ingredients:

- 2 cups broccoli florets
- 2 cups cauliflower florets
- 1 red bell pepper, cut into 1-inch pieces
- 2 carrots, sliced
- 2 tablespoons olive oil
- 3 garlic cloves, minced
- 1 teaspoon dried thyme
- 1 teaspoon dried rosemary
- Salt and pepper to taste

Instructions:

1. In a large bowl, combine all vegetables with olive oil, garlic, thyme, rosemary, salt, and pepper.
2. Preheat the air fryer to 380°F (193°C).
3. Cook the vegetable medley in the air fryer basket for 15 minutes, shaking halfway through, until vegetables are tender and slightly browned.
4. Serve hot.

Cooking Tips:

- Cutting the vegetables into similar-sized pieces will ensure even cooking.
- Add a sprinkle of grated Parmesan cheese before serving for a savory touch.

Air Fryer Shishito Peppers with Lemon Dip

Prep: 5 mins | Cook: 8 mins | Serves 4

Ingredients:

- 1 lb shishito peppers
- 1 tablespoon olive oil
- Salt to taste
- 1/2 cup sour cream or Greek yogurt
- 1 tablespoon lemon juice
- Zest of 1 lemon
- 1 garlic clove, minced
- Salt and pepper to taste

Instructions:

1. Toss shishito peppers with olive oil and salt.
2. Preheat the air fryer to 390°F (199°C).
3. Cook the peppers in the air fryer basket for 8 minutes, shaking occasionally, until blistered and tender.
4. Meanwhile, prepare the dip by combining sour cream or Greek yogurt with lemon juice, lemon zest, minced garlic, salt, and pepper.
5. Serve the peppers with the lemon dip on the side.

Cooking Tips:

- Watch the peppers closely as they cook quickly and can go from blistered to burnt.
- Pair the dip with other vegetables or chips for a versatile appetizer.

Air Fryer Buffalo Cauliflower Bites

Prep: 10 mins | Cook: 20 mins | Serves 4

Ingredients:

- 1 head of cauliflower, cut into bite-sized florets
- 1/2 cup buffalo sauce
- 1 tablespoon olive oil
- 1 teaspoon garlic powder
- 1/2 teaspoon paprika
- Salt and pepper to taste
- Ranch or blue cheese dressing for dipping

Instructions:

1. In a large bowl, toss cauliflower florets with olive oil, garlic powder, paprika, salt, and pepper.
2. Preheat the air fryer to 360°F (182°C).
3. Arrange the cauliflower in the air fryer basket and cook for 10 minutes.
4. Pour buffalo sauce over the cauliflower and toss to coat evenly.
5. Return the cauliflower to the air fryer and cook for an additional 10 minutes, or until crispy.
6. Serve with ranch or blue cheese dressing for dipping.

Cooking Tips:

- For extra crispy bites, let the cauliflower sit in the buffalo sauce for a few minutes before the second cook.
- For a lighter version, use a reduced-calorie buffalo sauce.

Air Fryer Roasted Root Vegetables

Prep: 15 mins | Cook: 18 mins | Serves 4

Ingredients:

- 2 carrots, peeled and sliced
- 2 parsnips, peeled and sliced
- 1 sweet potato, peeled and cubed
- 1 beet, peeled and cubed
- 2 tablespoons olive oil
- 1 teaspoon rosemary, chopped
- Salt and pepper to taste

Instructions:

1. In a large bowl, toss carrots, parsnips, sweet potato, and beet with olive oil, rosemary, salt, and pepper.
2. Preheat the air fryer to 380°F (193°C).
3. Cook the root vegetables in the air fryer basket for 18 minutes, shaking occasionally, until tender and slightly caramelized.
4. Serve warm as a side dish.

Cooking Tips:

- For an even roast, cut the vegetables into similar-sized pieces.
- Drizzle with honey before serving for a hint of sweetness.

Air Fryer Asparagus with Herbed Crumb Topping

Prep: 10 mins | Cook: 8 mins | Serves 4

Ingredients:

- 1 lb asparagus, trimmed
- 2 tablespoons olive oil
- 1/2 cup panko breadcrumbs
- 1 tablespoon fresh parsley, chopped
- 1 teaspoon fresh thyme leaves
- Zest of 1 lemon
- Salt and pepper to taste

Instructions:

1. Toss asparagus with 1 tablespoon of olive oil, salt, and pepper.
2. In a separate bowl, mix panko breadcrumbs, parsley, thyme, lemon zest, and remaining olive oil.
3. Preheat the air fryer to 360°F (182°C).
4. Arrange the asparagus in the air fryer basket and cook for 5 minutes.
5. Sprinkle the herbed crumb mixture over the asparagus and cook for an additional 3 minutes, or until the breadcrumbs are golden and the asparagus is tender.
6. Serve immediately.

Cooking Tips:

- Ensure the asparagus is not overcrowded in the basket for an even cook.
- Add grated Parmesan to the breadcrumb mixture for extra flavor.

Bacon-Wrapped Brussels Sprouts in Air Fryer

Prep: 15 mins | Cook: 12 mins | Serves 4

Ingredients:

- 16 Brussels sprouts
- 8 slices of bacon, cut in half
- 1 tablespoon maple syrup
- 1 tablespoon balsamic vinegar
- Pepper to taste

Instructions:

1. Wrap each Brussels sprout with a half slice of bacon and secure with a toothpick.
2. In a small bowl, mix together maple syrup and balsamic vinegar.
3. Preheat the air fryer to 390°F (199°C).
4. Brush the bacon-wrapped Brussels sprouts with the maple-balsamic mixture and sprinkle with pepper.
5. Cook in the air fryer for 12 minutes, or until the bacon is crisp and the Brussels sprouts are tender.
6. Serve immediately.

Cooking Tips:

- Cook in batches if necessary to avoid overcrowding, which can affect the crispness of the bacon.
- The toothpicks should be soaked in water before use to prevent burning.

Air Fryer Parsnip Fries with Spicy Mayo

Prep: 15 mins | Cook: 15 mins | Serves 4

Ingredients:

- 4 parsnips, peeled and cut into fries
- 2 tablespoons olive oil
- 1/2 teaspoon paprika
- Salt and pepper to taste
- 1/4 cup mayonnaise
- 1 tablespoon Sriracha or hot sauce
- Juice of 1/2 a lime

Instructions:

1. Toss parsnip fries with olive oil, paprika, salt, and pepper.
2. Preheat the air fryer to 400°F (204°C).
3. Cook parsnip fries in the air fryer basket for 15 minutes, shaking occasionally, until golden and crispy.
4. While fries are cooking, mix mayonnaise, Sriracha, and lime juice to create the spicy mayo.
5. Serve the fries hot with the spicy mayo on the side.

Cooking Tips:

- Don't overcrowd the air fryer basket; cook in batches for the crispiest results.
- For extra flavor, add garlic powder or onion powder to the fries before cooking.

Air Fryer Spiced Butternut Squash

Prep: 10 mins | Cook: 20 mins | Serves 4

Ingredients:

- 1 medium butternut squash, peeled and cubed
- 1 tablespoon olive oil
- 1 teaspoon cinnamon
- 1/2 teaspoon nutmeg
- 1/4 teaspoon cayenne pepper (optional)
- Salt to taste

Instructions:

1. Toss the butternut squash with olive oil, cinnamon, nutmeg, cayenne pepper, and salt.
2. Preheat the air fryer to 380°F (193°C).
3. Cook the squash in the air fryer basket for 20 minutes, shaking halfway through, until tender and slightly caramelized.
4. Serve as a side dish or as a healthy snack.

Cooking Tips:

- For a sweeter version, drizzle with honey before serving.
- Ensure cubes are cut evenly for consistent cooking.

Air Fryer Crispy Kale Chips

Prep: 5 mins | Cook: 6 mins | Serves 2

Ingredients:

- 1 bunch kale, leaves torn from stems and roughly chopped
- 1 tablespoon olive oil
- Salt to taste

Instructions:

1. Massage the kale with olive oil until each piece is lightly coated. Season with salt.
2. Preheat the air fryer to 360°F (182°C).
3. Cook the kale in the air fryer basket for 6 minutes, shaking occasionally, until crispy.
4. Serve immediately as a nutritious snack.

Cooking Tips:

- Kale shrinks significantly, so it's okay to fill the basket as long as there's room for air to circulate.
- For added flavor, sprinkle with nutritional yeast or garlic powder before cooking.

Air Fryer Stuffed Mushrooms with Cream Cheese

Prep: 15 mins | Cook: 10 mins | Serves 4

Ingredients:

- 12 large mushrooms, stems removed
- 1 cup cream cheese, softened
- 1/4 cup grated Parmesan cheese
- 1 garlic clove, minced
- 1 tablespoon chives, chopped
- Salt and pepper to taste

Instructions:

1. In a bowl, combine cream cheese, Parmesan, garlic, chives, salt, and pepper.
2. Fill each mushroom cap with the cream cheese mixture.
3. Preheat the air fryer to 350°F (177°C).
4. Cook the stuffed mushrooms in the air fryer basket for 10 minutes or until the mushrooms are tender and the tops are slightly golden.
5. Serve warm as an appetizer or side dish.

Cooking Tips:

- Wipe the mushrooms with a damp cloth instead of washing them to prevent them from becoming soggy.
- Experiment with different herbs like parsley or dill for varied flavors.

Air Fryer Balsamic Glazed Eggplant Steaks

Prep: 10 mins | Cook: 12 mins | Serves 4

Ingredients:

- 2 large eggplants, sliced into 1/2 inch thick rounds
- 2 tablespoons olive oil
- 2 tablespoons balsamic vinegar
- Salt and pepper to taste
- Fresh parsley, chopped (for garnish)

Instructions:

1. Brush each eggplant slice with olive oil and season with salt and pepper.
2. Preheat the air fryer to 380°F (193°C).
3. Cook the eggplant slices in the air fryer basket for 12 minutes, flipping halfway through, until tender and slightly browned.
4. Drizzle balsamic vinegar over the cooked eggplant steaks before serving.
5. Garnish with fresh parsley.

Cooking Tips:

- Do not overcrowd the air fryer basket to ensure even cooking.
- For a more substantial glaze, reduce the balsamic vinegar on the stove until thickened, then brush on the eggplant after air frying.

Air Fryer Corn Ribs with Smoky Rub

Prep: 10 mins | Cook: 10 mins | Serves 4

Ingredients:

- 4 ears of corn, shucked and quartered lengthwise
- 1 tablespoon olive oil
- 1 teaspoon smoked paprika
- 1/2 teaspoon garlic powder
- 1/2 teaspoon onion powder
- 1/4 teaspoon cumin
- Salt and pepper to taste

Instructions:

1. Brush the corn ribs with olive oil.
2. Mix smoked paprika, garlic powder, onion powder, cumin, salt, and pepper. Sprinkle the mixture over the corn.
3. Preheat the air fryer to 400°F (204°C).
4. Cook the corn ribs in the air fryer basket for 10 minutes, flipping halfway through, until charred and tender.
5. Serve as a side with your favorite dipping sauce.

Cooking Tips:

- Use a sharp knife to cut the corn into ribs to prevent them from breaking.
- For an extra kick, add a pinch of cayenne pepper to the rub.

Chapter 4: Snacks, Sandwiches, and Appetizers

Air-Fryer Pickles

Prep: 10 mins | Cook: 8 mins | Serves 4

Ingredients:

- 1 cup dill pickle slices, drained and patted dry
- 1/2 cup all-purpose flour
- 1 egg, beaten
- 1 cup panko breadcrumbs
- 1 teaspoon garlic powder
- 1/2 teaspoon paprika
- Salt and pepper to taste

Instructions:

1. Create a breading station with three bowls: one with flour, one with beaten egg, and one with panko mixed with garlic powder, paprika, salt, and pepper.
2. Dip each pickle slice into the flour, then egg, and finally coat with the panko mixture.
3. Preheat the air fryer to 400°F (204°C).
4. Cook the breaded pickles in a single layer in the air fryer basket for 8 minutes, flipping halfway through, until golden brown and crispy.
5. Serve with ranch dressing or your favorite dipping sauce.

Cooking Tips:

- Ensure the pickles are dry before breading to help the coating stick better.
- Spray the pickles lightly with cooking spray before air frying for extra crispiness.

Air-Fryer Tortilla Chips

Prep: 5 mins | Cook: 5 mins | Serves 4

Ingredients:

- 8 corn tortillas, cut into wedges
- 1 tablespoon olive oil
- Salt to taste
- Optional: chili powder or lime zest for seasoning

Instructions:

1. Toss tortilla wedges with olive oil and salt, and add additional seasonings if desired.
2. Preheat the air fryer to 350°F (177°C).
3. Cook the tortilla wedges in the air fryer basket for 5 minutes, shaking once, until they are crispy and lightly golden.
4. Serve with salsa, guacamole, or your favorite dip.

Cooking Tips:

- Do not overcrowd the air fryer; cook in batches for even crisping.
- Watch closely as they can burn quickly.

Air-Fryer Stuffed Jalapeños

Prep: 15 mins | Cook: 10 mins | Serves 4

Ingredients:

- 8 jalapeños, halved and seeded
- 4 ounces cream cheese, softened
- 1/2 cup shredded cheddar cheese
- 1/4 cup green onions, chopped
- 1/2 teaspoon garlic powder
- Salt and pepper to taste
- 1/4 cup crumbled bacon (optional)

Instructions:

1. In a bowl, mix cream cheese, cheddar cheese, green onions, garlic powder, salt, and pepper. Stir in bacon if using.
2. Stuff each jalapeño half with the mixture.
3. Preheat the air fryer to 370°F (188°C).
4. Cook the stuffed jalapeños in the air fryer basket for 10 minutes, or until the cheese is melted and bubbly.
5. Serve warm as a spicy and cheesy appetizer.

Cooking Tips:

- Wear gloves when handling jalapeños to avoid irritation.
- If you prefer less heat, soak the jalapeño halves in milk for an hour before stuffing.

Air-Fryer Crispy Chickpeas

Prep: 5 mins | Cook: 15 mins | Serves 4

Ingredients:

- 1 can (15 oz) chickpeas, drained, rinsed, and patted dry
- 1 tablespoon olive oil
- 1/2 teaspoon smoked paprika
- 1/4 teaspoon cumin
- Salt to taste

Instructions:

1. Toss chickpeas with olive oil, smoked paprika, cumin, and salt.
2. Preheat the air fryer to 390°F (199°C).
3. Cook the chickpeas in the air fryer basket for 15 minutes, shaking occasionally, until crispy and golden.
4. Enjoy as a crunchy snack or a topping for salads.

Cooking Tips:

- Make sure chickpeas are thoroughly dried to achieve the best crispiness.
- Experiment with different spices like chili powder or curry powder for variety.

Air-Fryer Mini Calzones

Prep: 20 mins | Cook: 10 mins | Serves 4

Ingredients:

- 1 pound pizza dough, divided into 8 pieces
- 1/2 cup pizza sauce
- 1 cup shredded mozzarella cheese
- Your choice of fillings: cooked sausage, pepperoni, vegetables
- 1 beaten egg for egg wash

Instructions:

1. Roll out each piece of dough into a small circle.
2. On one half of each circle, spread pizza sauce, mozzarella, and your chosen fillings.
3. Fold the dough over the filling to create a half-moon shape. Seal edges with a fork.
4. Brush each calzone with egg wash.
5. Preheat the air fryer to 360°F (182°C).
6. Cook the mini calzones in the air fryer basket for 10 minutes, or until golden brown.
7. Serve with extra pizza sauce for dipping.

Cooking Tips:

- Don't overfill the calzones to prevent them from opening during cooking.
- Rotate the calzones halfway through cooking for even browning.

Air-Fryer Coconut Shrimp with Piña Colada Dipping Sauce

Prep: 15 mins | Cook: 8 mins | Serves 4

Ingredients:

- 1 lb large shrimp, peeled and deveined
- 1/2 cup all-purpose flour
- 1/2 teaspoon salt
- 1/4 teaspoon black pepper
- 2 large eggs, beaten
- 1 cup panko breadcrumbs
- 1 cup shredded coconut
- Cooking spray

For the Piña Colada Dipping Sauce:

- 1/2 cup canned coconut cream
- 1/4 cup crushed pineapple
- 2 tablespoons pineapple juice
- 1 tablespoon sugar
- 1 teaspoon rum extract (optional)

Instructions:

1. Set up three bowls for dredging: one with flour mixed with salt and pepper, one with beaten eggs, and one with a mixture of panko breadcrumbs and shredded coconut.
2. Dip each shrimp first in the flour, then the egg, and lastly in the coconut mixture.
3. Spray the shrimp lightly with cooking spray.
4. Preheat the air fryer to 400°F (204°C).
5. Cook the shrimp in the air fryer for 8 minutes, flipping halfway through, until golden and crispy.
6. For the sauce, combine coconut cream, crushed pineapple, pineapple juice, sugar, and rum extract in a bowl.
7. Serve the shrimp immediately with the piña colada sauce.

Cooking Tips:

- Press the coconut mixture onto the shrimp to ensure it adheres well.
- Make sure not to overcrowd the air fryer basket to allow for even cooking.

Air-Fryer Buffalo Chicken Wings

Prep: 10 mins | Cook: 25 mins | Serves 4

Ingredients:

- 2 lbs chicken wings, split and tips removed
- 1 tablespoon baking powder
- 1/2 teaspoon salt
- 1/2 cup buffalo wing sauce
- 2 tablespoons unsalted butter, melted
- Ranch or blue cheese dressing for serving

Instructions:

1. Pat the chicken wings dry and toss with baking powder and salt.
2. Preheat the air fryer to 400°F (204°C).
3. Cook the wings in the air fryer for 25 minutes, flipping halfway through, until crispy.
4. Combine the buffalo wing sauce and melted butter.
5. Toss the cooked wings in the sauce to coat.
6. Serve with ranch or blue cheese dressing and celery sticks.

Cooking Tips:

- The baking powder helps to make the skin extra crispy.
- Adjust the heat level by using a milder or hotter buffalo sauce as preferred.

Air-Fryer Ham and Cheese Sliders

Prep: 10 mins | Cook: 10 mins | Serves 4

Ingredients:

- 12 slider buns
- 12 slices of ham
- 12 slices of cheese (Swiss, cheddar, or your choice)
- 2 tablespoons mustard
- 2 tablespoons honey
- 1/2 cup butter, melted
- 1 teaspoon poppy seeds

Instructions:

1. Cut the slider buns in half and layer with ham and cheese.
2. Mix the mustard and honey into the melted butter and pour over the assembled sliders.
3. Sprinkle with poppy seeds.
4. Preheat the air fryer to 350°F (177°C).
5. Cook the sliders in the air fryer for 10 minutes until the cheese is melted and buns are golden brown.
6. Serve warm.

Cooking Tips:

- Cover the sliders with aluminum foil during the first half of cooking to prevent the tops from burning.
- For a variation, add a slice of pineapple for a Hawaiian twist.

Air-Fryer Garlic Parmesan Knots

Prep: 15 mins | Cook: 6 mins | Serves 4

Ingredients:

- 1 can (16 oz) refrigerated biscuit dough
- 1/4 cup grated Parmesan cheese
- 3 tablespoons unsalted butter, melted
- 1/2 teaspoon garlic powder
- 1 teaspoon dried parsley

Instructions:

1. Tie each biscuit into a knot and place in the air fryer basket.
2. Mix melted butter with garlic powder and parsley.
3. Brush the butter mixture over the knots.
4. Sprinkle with Parmesan cheese.
5. Preheat the air fryer to 330°F (165°C).
6. Cook the knots for 6 minutes until golden brown.
7. Serve warm as a side or appetizer.

Cooking Tips:

- Don't overcrowd the air fryer; cook in batches if needed.
- Serve with marinara sauce for dipping.

Air-Fryer Mozzarella Sticks

Prep: 15 mins (plus freezing) | Cook: 6 mins | Serves 4

Ingredients:

- 12 mozzarella cheese sticks
- 1/2 cup all-purpose flour
- 1 large egg, beaten
- 1 cup Italian breadcrumbs
- 1 teaspoon Italian seasoning
- Cooking spray

Instructions:

1. Freeze the cheese sticks for at least 2 hours.
2. Coat the frozen cheese sticks in flour, dip into the egg, and then roll in a mixture of breadcrumbs and Italian seasoning.
3. Spray the coated cheese sticks with cooking spray.
4. Preheat the air fryer to 390°F (199°C).
5. Cook the mozzarella sticks for 6 minutes, turning halfway through, until golden and crispy.
6. Serve immediately with marinara sauce for dipping.

Cooking Tips:

- Freezing the cheese sticks before cooking helps prevent the cheese from oozing out during the cooking process.
- Ensure the cheese sticks are fully coated with breadcrumbs to prevent sticking to the air fryer basket.

Air-Fryer Avocado Fries

Prep: 10 mins | Cook: 8 mins | Serves 4

Ingredients:

- 2 large avocados, sliced into wedges
- 1/2 cup all-purpose flour
- 1 teaspoon chili powder
- Salt and pepper to taste
- 2 large eggs, beaten
- 1 cup panko breadcrumbs
- Cooking spray

Instructions:

1. In a bowl, mix flour with chili powder, salt, and pepper.
2. Dip avocado slices in flour, then in beaten eggs, and finally coat with panko breadcrumbs.
3. Spray the avocado fries with cooking spray.
4. Preheat the air fryer to 400°F (204°C).
5. Arrange the avocado fries in the air fryer basket in a single layer and cook for 8 minutes, until crispy and golden.
6. Serve with your favorite dipping sauce, such as ranch or spicy mayo.

Cooking Tips:

- For extra crispiness, you can spray the avocado fries once more halfway through the cooking time.
- Handle the avocado slices gently to keep them from breaking apart.

Air-Fryer Mini Monte Cristo Sandwiches

Prep: 15 mins | Cook: 4 mins | Serves 4

Ingredients:

- 8 slices of white or brioche bread, crusts trimmed
- 4 slices of deli ham
- 4 slices of turkey
- 4 slices of Swiss cheese
- 1/4 cup mayonnaise
- 1/4 cup raspberry or strawberry jam
- 2 large eggs
- 1/2 cup milk
- Powdered sugar for dusting

Instructions:

1. Spread mayonnaise on four slices of bread and jam on the other four slices.
2. Make sandwiches with ham, turkey, and cheese in between the slices.
3. In a bowl, whisk together eggs and milk.
4. Dip each sandwich into the egg mixture, coating both sides.
5. Preheat the air fryer to 360°F (182°C).
6. Cook the sandwiches for 4 minutes, flipping halfway through, until golden brown and the cheese is melted.
7. Dust with powdered sugar before serving.

Cooking Tips:

- Press the sandwiches slightly to ensure they hold together while cooking.
- Serve immediately for the best taste and texture.

Air-Fryer Loaded Potato Skins

Prep: 10 mins | Cook: 15 mins | Serves 4

Ingredients:

- 4 large russet potatoes, cooked and halved
- 1/2 cup shredded cheddar cheese
- 4 slices bacon, cooked and crumbled
- 1/4 cup green onions, sliced
- Sour cream, for serving

Instructions:

1. Scoop out the center of each potato half, leaving a small margin of potato on the skins.
2. Sprinkle the insides with cheese and bacon crumbles.
3. Preheat the air fryer to 400°F (204°C).
4. Place potato skins in the air fryer and cook for 5 minutes or until the cheese is melted and skins are crispy.
5. Garnish with green onions and serve with sour cream on the side.

Cooking Tips:

- Make sure to pre-cook the potatoes until they're just done as they will crisp up in the air fryer.
- For a healthier version, use turkey bacon and low-fat cheese.

Air-Fryer Crispy Ravioli

Prep: 10 mins | Cook: 8 mins | Serves 4

Ingredients:

- 1 package (9 oz) refrigerated ravioli
- 1/2 cup grated Parmesan cheese
- 1/2 cup Italian breadcrumbs
- 2 large eggs, beaten
- Marinara sauce, for serving

Instructions:

1. Combine Parmesan cheese and breadcrumbs in a shallow dish.
2. Dip each ravioli in the beaten eggs, then coat with the breadcrumb mixture.
3. Preheat the air fryer to 350°F (177°C).
4. Cook the ravioli in batches for 4 minutes, flipping halfway through, until golden brown and crispy.
5. Serve with marinara sauce for dipping.

Cooking Tips:

- Don't stack the ravioli in the air fryer to ensure they cook evenly.
- For extra flavor, mix some dried herbs into the breadcrumb mixture.

Air-Fryer BBQ Chicken Pizza Pockets

Prep: 20 mins | Cook: 10 mins | Serves 4

Ingredients:

- 1 can (13.8 oz) refrigerated pizza dough
- 1/2 cup BBQ sauce
- 1 cup cooked chicken, shredded
- 1/2 cup red onion, thinly sliced
- 1 cup mozzarella cheese, shredded
- 1 beaten egg, for egg wash
- Cooking spray

Instructions:

1. Roll out pizza dough and cut into 8 equal squares.
2. On each square, spread BBQ sauce, and top with chicken, onion, and cheese.
3. Fold the dough over the filling to create a pocket, crimp the edges with a fork to seal.
4. Brush the tops with egg wash and spray lightly with cooking spray.
5. Preheat the air fryer to 350°F (177°C).
6. Cook the pizza pockets for 10 minutes, until the dough is golden brown and cooked through.
7. Serve hot with extra BBQ sauce if desired.

Cooking Tips:

- Ensure the edges are sealed well to prevent the filling from leaking out.
- You can add a little bit of cilantro or parsley to the filling for extra flavor.

Air-Fryer Grilled Cheese Sandwich

Prep: 5 mins | Cook: 8 mins | Serves 2

Ingredients:

- 4 slices of bread (your choice)
- 2 tablespoons butter, softened
- 4 slices of cheddar cheese (or cheese of choice)
- Cooking spray (optional)

Instructions:

1. Spread butter on one side of each bread slice.
2. Place two slices of cheese between two slices of bread with the buttered sides facing out.
3. Preheat the air fryer to 370°F (188°C).
4. Spray the air fryer basket with cooking spray if desired, and place the sandwich in the basket.
5. Cook for 4 minutes, flip the sandwich, and cook for an additional 4 minutes or until the bread is toasted to your preference and the cheese is melted.
6. Serve immediately.

Cooking Tips:

- Use a toothpick to secure the sandwich if needed to prevent the bread from flying up due to the air fryer's fan.
- For a gourmet twist, try using a combination of cheeses and add a slice of tomato or a sprinkle of dried herbs.

Air-Fryer Meatball Subs

Prep: 10 mins | Cook: 10 mins | Serves 4

Ingredients:

- 4 sub rolls, split open but not all the way through
- 16 cooked meatballs
- 1 cup marinara sauce, warmed
- 1 cup shredded mozzarella cheese
- 1 tablespoon grated Parmesan cheese
- 1 teaspoon Italian seasoning
- Cooking spray

Instructions:

1. Place 4 meatballs in each sub roll.
2. Spoon marinara sauce over the meatballs.
3. Sprinkle with mozzarella, Parmesan cheese, and Italian seasoning.
4. Preheat the air fryer to 360°F (182°C).
5. Place the subs in the air fryer basket and cook for 5 minutes or until the cheese is melted and bubbly and the rolls are crispy.
6. Serve hot.

Cooking Tips:

- If your meatballs are not pre-cooked, cook them in the air fryer first at 400°F for about 10 minutes before adding to the subs.
- For a toasted top, open the subs after cooking, sprinkle with cheese, and air fry for an additional 2 minutes.

Air-Fryer Chicken Caprese Paninis

Prep: 10 mins | Cook: 8 mins | Serves 4

Ingredients:

- 4 ciabatta rolls, sliced in half
- 1 cup cooked chicken breast, sliced
- 1 large tomato, sliced
- 4 ounces fresh mozzarella cheese, sliced
- Fresh basil leaves
- Balsamic glaze
- Salt and pepper to taste
- Cooking spray

Instructions:

1. Assemble the paninis by layering chicken, tomato slices, mozzarella, and basil leaves on the bottom half of each ciabatta roll. Drizzle with balsamic glaze and season with salt and pepper.
2. Top with the other half of the ciabatta rolls.
3. Preheat the air fryer to 360°F (182°C).
4. Spray the air fryer basket with cooking spray and place the paninis inside.
5. Cook for 8 minutes, flipping halfway through, or until the cheese is melted and the bread is toasted.
6. Serve warm with extra balsamic glaze on the side if desired.

Cooking Tips:

- Press down on the paninis slightly before cooking to help them heat evenly.
- If you have a panini press, you can use it to press the sandwiches while they cook in the air fryer.

Air-Fryer Veggie Spring Rolls

Prep: 20 mins | Cook: 8 mins | Serves 4

Ingredients:

- 8 spring roll wrappers
- 1 cup shredded cabbage
- 1/2 cup grated carrots
- 1/2 cup thinly sliced bell peppers
- 1/4 cup fresh cilantro leaves
- 2 tablespoons soy sauce
- 1 teaspoon sesame oil
- Cooking spray

Instructions:

1. In a bowl, mix the cabbage, carrots, bell peppers, cilantro, soy sauce, and sesame oil.
2. Soften the spring roll wrappers as per the package instructions.
3. Place a portion of the veggie mixture on each wrapper and roll tightly, tucking in the edges.
4. Preheat the air fryer to 390°F (199°C).
5. Place the spring rolls in the air fryer basket, seam-side down, and spray lightly with cooking spray.
6. Cook for 8 minutes, turning halfway through, until they are golden brown and crispy.
7. Serve with a dipping sauce of your choice.

Cooking Tips:

- Do not overcrowd the air fryer basket; cook in batches if necessary.
- Keep the rolled spring rolls under a damp cloth to prevent them from drying out before cooking.

Air-Fryer Cinnamon Apple Chips

Prep: 15 mins | Cook: 15 mins | Serves 2

Ingredients:

- 2 large apples, thinly sliced
- 1 teaspoon ground cinnamon
- 1 tablespoon granulated sugar (optional)

Instructions:

1. In a bowl, toss the apple slices with cinnamon and sugar until evenly coated.
2. Arrange the apple slices in a single layer in the air fryer basket.
3. Preheat the air fryer to 300°F (149°C).
4. Cook for 7-8 minutes, flip the apple slices, and continue cooking for another 7-8 minutes or until crisp.
5. Let the apple chips cool to become crisper.
6. Serve as a snack or garnish.

Cooking Tips:

- For best results, use a mandolin to slice the apples evenly.
- Monitor the chips closely towards the end to prevent burning, as the cooking time may vary depending on the thickness of the slices.

Chapter 5: Desserts

Air Fryer Salted Caramel Apple Crumble

Prep: 15 mins | Cook: 15 mins | Serves 4

Ingredients:

- 2 large apples, peeled, cored, and chopped
- 1/4 cup salted caramel sauce
- 1/2 cup all-purpose flour
- 1/4 cup rolled oats
- 1/4 cup brown sugar
- 1/4 cup unsalted butter, chilled and diced
- 1/2 teaspoon ground cinnamon
- Pinch of salt

Instructions:

1. Toss the chopped apples with half of the salted caramel sauce.
2. In a separate bowl, mix the flour, oats, brown sugar, cinnamon, and salt. Add the butter and rub into the dry ingredients until crumbly.
3. Place the apple mixture in a baking dish that fits in your air fryer basket. Top with the crumble mixture.
4. Spray the top with a light coating of cooking spray to help it brown.
5. Preheat the air fryer to 350°F (177°C).
6. Air fry the apple crumble for 12-15 minutes until the topping is golden brown and the apples are tender.
7. Drizzle with the remaining salted caramel sauce before serving.

Cooking Tips:

- If the crumble starts to brown too quickly, cover it with aluminum foil.
- Serve with a scoop of vanilla ice cream for extra indulgence.

Air Fryer Chocolate-Stuffed Churro Bites

Prep: 20 mins | Cook: 8 mins | Serves 4

Ingredients:

- 1 tube refrigerated biscuit dough
- 8 small pieces of chocolate or chocolate chips
- 1/4 cup sugar
- 1 teaspoon ground cinnamon
- Cooking spray

Instructions:

1. Flatten each biscuit and place a piece of chocolate in the center. Wrap the dough around the chocolate and seal, forming a ball.
2. In a small bowl, combine sugar and cinnamon.
3. Preheat the air fryer to 360°F (182°C).
4. Spray the air fryer basket with cooking spray and place the dough balls inside, leaving space between each one.
5. Air fry for 6-8 minutes until the balls are puffed and golden.
6. Immediately roll the churro bites in the cinnamon-sugar mixture until well coated.
7. Serve warm.

Cooking Tips:

- Ensure the dough is sealed tightly around the chocolate to prevent leaking.
- The churro bites are best enjoyed fresh but can be reheated in the air fryer for 2-3 minutes.

Air Fryer Lemon Ricotta Cheesecake

Prep: 10 mins | Cook: 20 mins | Serves 4

Ingredients:

- 1 cup ricotta cheese
- 1/4 cup granulated sugar
- Zest of 1 lemon
- 1 tablespoon lemon juice
- 1 egg
- 1/4 cup all-purpose flour
- 1 teaspoon vanilla extract

Instructions:

1. In a bowl, mix together ricotta, sugar, lemon zest, lemon juice, and vanilla extract until smooth.
2. Beat in the egg, then fold in the flour until just combined.
3. Pour the mixture into a greased springform pan that fits in your air fryer.
4. Preheat the air fryer to 300°F (149°C).
5. Air fry the cheesecake for 15-20 minutes until set but still slightly jiggly in the center.
6. Let it cool to room temperature, then chill in the refrigerator before serving.

Cooking Tips:

- Wrap the bottom of the springform pan in foil to catch any drips.
- Top with fresh berries or a dollop of whipped cream before serving.

Air Fryer Banana Caramel Spring Rolls

Prep: 15 mins | Cook: 8 mins | Serves 4

Ingredients:

- 4 bananas
- 8 spring roll wrappers
- 1/2 cup caramel sauce
- Powdered sugar for dusting
- Cooking spray

Instructions:

1. Place a banana on each spring roll wrapper and drizzle with caramel sauce.
2. Roll up the wrapper, tucking in the ends, and seal with a little water.
3. Preheat the air fryer to 390°F (199°C).
4. Spray the air fryer basket with cooking spray and place the spring rolls in the basket.
5. Air fry for 6-8 minutes until golden brown and crispy.
6. Dust with powdered sugar and serve with extra caramel sauce for dipping.

Cooking Tips:

- Don't overload the spring rolls with caramel sauce to prevent leaking during cooking.
- Serve immediately while the spring rolls are crispy and warm.

Air Fryer Spiced Maple Pumpkin Seeds

Prep: 5 mins | Cook: 10 mins | Serves 2

Ingredients:

- 1 cup raw pumpkin seeds
- 1 tablespoon maple syrup
- 1/2 teaspoon ground cinnamon
- 1/4 teaspoon ground nutmeg
- Pinch of salt

Instructions:

1. In a bowl, toss the pumpkin seeds with maple syrup, cinnamon, nutmeg, and salt until evenly coated.
2. Spread the seeds in a single layer in the air fryer basket.
3. Preheat the air fryer to 330°F (165°C).
4. Cook for 8-10 minutes, stirring halfway through, until the seeds are toasted and crispy.
5. Let them cool before serving.

Cooking Tips:

- Stir the pumpkin seeds occasionally during cooking for even toasting.
- Watch closely to prevent burning, as seeds can go from toasted to burnt quickly.

Air Fryer Pecan Pie Clusters

Prep: 10 mins | Cook: 6 mins | Serves 4

Ingredients:

- 1 cup pecans, roughly chopped
- 1/4 cup corn syrup
- 1/4 cup brown sugar
- 1 teaspoon vanilla extract
- Pinch of salt
- 1/2 teaspoon ground cinnamon

Instructions:

1. In a bowl, combine the pecans, corn syrup, brown sugar, vanilla extract, salt, and cinnamon. Mix until the pecans are well coated.
2. Spoon small clusters of the pecan mixture onto a parchment-lined air fryer basket, ensuring they are not touching.
3. Preheat the air fryer to 300°F (149°C).
4. Cook the pecan clusters for 5-6 minutes until they are caramelized and have a sticky coating.
5. Allow to cool slightly; they will harden as they cool.

Cooking Tips:

- Use a silicone mat or parchment paper to prevent sticking.
- Serve as a sweet snack or dessert topping.

Air Fryer Toasted Coconut Lime Bars

Prep: 15 mins | Cook: 12 mins | Serves 4

Ingredients:

- 1 cup graham cracker crumbs
- 1/4 cup melted butter
- 1/4 cup sugar
- 1/2 cup toasted coconut flakes
- 1 lime, zested and juiced
- 1 (8 oz) package cream cheese, softened
- 1/4 cup condensed milk

Instructions:

1. Mix graham cracker crumbs, melted butter, and sugar to form the crust mixture.
2. Press the crumb mixture into the bottom of a pan that fits into your air fryer.
3. In another bowl, beat together the cream cheese, condensed milk, lime zest, and lime juice until smooth.
4. Spread the cream cheese mixture over the crust and sprinkle with toasted coconut flakes.
5. Preheat the air fryer to 320°F (160°C).
6. Cook for 10-12 minutes until the edges are golden and the center is set.
7. Allow to cool before slicing into bars.

Cooking Tips:

- Chill in the fridge for an hour before serving for a firmer texture.
- Use fresh lime juice for the best flavor.

Air Fryer Blackberry Cobbler Pockets

Prep: 15 mins | Cook: 10 mins | Serves 4

Ingredients:

- 1 cup blackberries
- 2 tablespoons sugar
- 1 teaspoon lemon zest
- 1 package refrigerated pie crusts
- 1 egg, beaten (for egg wash)
- Additional sugar for sprinkling

Instructions:

1. Toss blackberries with sugar and lemon zest.
2. Cut the pie crusts into circles or squares.
3. Place a spoonful of the blackberry mixture into the center of each pie crust piece.
4. Fold over the crust and press the edges with a fork to seal.
5. Brush the tops of the pockets with egg wash and sprinkle with sugar.
6. Preheat the air fryer to 350°F (177°C).
7. Cook the cobbler pockets for 8-10 minutes until golden and bubbly.
8. Serve warm with ice cream or whipped cream.

Cooking Tips:

- Make sure to seal the edges well to prevent the filling from leaking out.
- Adjust the amount of sugar based on the sweetness of the blackberries.

Air Fryer Cardamom Pear Tarts

Prep: 20 mins | Cook: 15 mins | Serves 4

Ingredients:

- 2 pears, thinly sliced
- 1/4 cup brown sugar
- 1/2 teaspoon ground cardamom
- 1 package puff pastry, thawed
- 1 egg, beaten (for egg wash)

Instructions:

1. Toss pear slices with brown sugar and cardamom.
2. Cut the puff pastry into squares.
3. Arrange the pear slices in the center of each pastry square.
4. Fold the edges of the pastry over the pears slightly.
5. Brush the pastry with egg wash.
6. Preheat the air fryer to 350°F (177°C).
7. Air fry the tarts for 12-15 minutes until puffed and golden.
8. Serve warm with a dollop of cream or a sprinkle of powdered sugar.

Cooking Tips:

- Do not overlap the pear slices too much to ensure they cook evenly.
- Serve immediately for the best texture of the puff pastry.

Air Fryer Mini Matcha Cheesecakes

Prep: 20 mins | Cook: 15 mins | Serves 4

Ingredients:

- 1/2 cup graham cracker crumbs
- 2 tablespoons melted butter
- 8 oz cream cheese, softened
- 1/4 cup sugar
- 1 tablespoon matcha powder
- 1 egg
- 1 teaspoon vanilla extract

Instructions:

1. Mix graham cracker crumbs and melted butter. Press into the bottom of mini cheesecake pans that fit in your air fryer.
2. Beat the cream cheese, sugar, matcha powder, egg, and vanilla until smooth.
3. Pour the matcha mixture over the crusts in the pans.
4. Preheat the air fryer to 300°F (149°C).
5. Cook the cheesecakes for 12-15 minutes until set but slightly wobbly in the center.
6. Let them cool, then chill in the refrigerator for at least 2 hours before serving.

Cooking Tips:

- If the air fryer is too hot, the tops may crack, so it's better to cook at a lower temperature for a bit longer.
- A water bath is not necessary in the air fryer, but ensure there's enough space around each cheesecake for even cooking.

Air Fryer Cinnamon Roll Bites

Prep: 10 mins | Cook: 8 mins | Serves 4

Ingredients:

- 1 can refrigerated cinnamon roll dough
- 1 tablespoon melted butter
- 2 tablespoons granulated sugar
- 1 teaspoon ground cinnamon
- Cream cheese icing (included with cinnamon roll dough)

Instructions:

1. Cut each cinnamon roll into quarters.
2. In a bowl, mix together the granulated sugar and ground cinnamon.
3. Toss the dough pieces in the melted butter, then roll them in the cinnamon-sugar mixture.
4. Place the coated pieces in the air fryer basket in a single layer, ensuring they do not touch.
5. Preheat the air fryer to 360°F (182°C).
6. Cook for 6-8 minutes until the bites are puffed up and golden brown.
7. Drizzle with cream cheese icing while still warm.

Cooking Tips:

- Do not overcrowd the air fryer basket; cook in batches if necessary.
- Serve immediately for best results, as they are best when warm.

Air Fryer Honey Glazed Fig Pastry

Prep: 15 mins | Cook: 10 mins | Serves 4

Ingredients:

- 1 sheet puff pastry, thawed
- 8 fresh figs, quartered
- 1/4 cup honey
- 1 tablespoon lemon juice
- 1/4 teaspoon ground cinnamon
- Powdered sugar for dusting

Instructions:

1. Cut the puff pastry into squares or rectangles.
2. Top each piece of pastry with a few fig quarters.
3. Mix honey, lemon juice, and cinnamon together, and drizzle over the figs.
4. Preheat the air fryer to 350°F (177°C).
5. Place the pastries in the air fryer basket, not touching, and cook for 8-10 minutes until puffed and golden.
6. Dust with powdered sugar before serving.

Cooking Tips:

- The pastries can be brushed with a bit of beaten egg before cooking for extra shine.
- Keep a close eye to prevent the pastry from over-browning.

Air Fryer Cherry Chocolate Bombolini

Prep: 20 mins | Cook: 10 mins | Serves 4

Ingredients:

- 1 can refrigerated biscuit dough
- 1/2 cup cherry jam
- 1/4 cup chocolate chips
- Powdered sugar for dusting
- 1/4 cup milk (for glaze)
- 1/2 cup powdered sugar (for glaze)

Instructions:

1. Flatten each biscuit dough piece and place a teaspoon of cherry jam and a few chocolate chips in the center.
2. Enclose the filling with the dough and roll into a ball.
3. Preheat the air fryer to 350°F (177°C).
4. Cook the bombolini for 8-10 minutes until golden brown.
5. Mix 1/2 cup powdered sugar and milk to make a glaze.
6. While still warm, dip each bombolini in the glaze and then dust with powdered sugar.

Cooking Tips:

Ensure the edges are sealed tightly to prevent the filling from leaking out.
Serve warm for a gooey chocolate center.

Air Fryer Almond Joy Bites

Prep: 15 mins | Cook: 6 mins | Serves 4

Ingredients:

- 1 cup shredded coconut
- 3 tablespoons condensed milk
- 12 whole almonds
- 1/2 cup melted milk chocolate

Instructions:

1. Mix the shredded coconut with condensed milk to form a sticky mixture.
2. Take a small amount of the coconut mixture, press an almond into the center, and roll into a ball.
3. Dip each coconut ball into the melted chocolate to coat.
4. Chill in the refrigerator for 10 minutes to set the chocolate slightly.
5. Preheat the air fryer to 320°F (160°C).
6. Cook the bites for 4-6 minutes until the coconut is toasted.
7. Let cool before serving.

Cooking Tips:

- Chill the coconut balls before air frying if they are too soft.
- Use parchment paper in the air fryer basket to prevent sticking.

Air Fryer Raspberry Almond Twists

Prep: 20 mins | Cook: 12 mins | Serves 4

Ingredients:

- 1 sheet puff pastry, thawed
- 1/4 cup raspberry jam
- 1/4 cup cream cheese, softened
- 1/4 cup sliced almonds
- Powdered sugar for dusting

Instructions:

1. Cut the puff pastry into strips.
2. Spread a thin layer of cream cheese and raspberry jam on each strip.
3. Twist the strips and sprinkle with sliced almonds.
4. Preheat the air fryer to 360°F (182°C).
5. Cook for 10-12 minutes until golden and puffed up.
6. Dust with powdered sugar before serving.

Cooking Tips:

- Don't overload with filling to prevent it from spilling out during cooking.
- If the pastry starts to brown too quickly, lower the temperature by 10-15 degrees.

Air Fryer Orange Pistachio Baklava

Prep: 30 mins | Cook: 15 mins | Serves 6

Ingredients:

- 1 package phyllo dough, thawed
- 1 cup chopped pistachios
- 1/2 cup melted butter
- 1 teaspoon grated orange zest
- 1/2 cup sugar
- 1/2 cup water
- 1/4 cup honey
- 1 tablespoon orange juice

Instructions:

1. Brush each phyllo sheet with melted butter and layer them, sprinkling chopped pistachios and orange zest between each layer.
2. Cut the layered sheets into squares or triangles and place them in the air fryer basket.
3. Preheat the air fryer to 350°F (177°C).
4. Cook for 12-15 minutes until golden and crispy.
5. Meanwhile, make a syrup by boiling sugar, water, honey, and orange juice until thickened.
6. Drizzle the syrup over the hot baklava after it's cooked.

Cooking Tips:

Keep the phyllo dough covered with a damp towel while working to prevent it from drying out.

Syrup should be made ahead of time and cooled so it doesn't make the pastry soggy.

Air Fryer Strawberry Basil Galettes

Prep: 20 mins | Cook: 15 mins | Serves 4

Ingredients:

- 1 sheet puff pastry, thawed
- 1 cup sliced strawberries
- 2 tablespoons chopped fresh basil
- 1 tablespoon sugar
- 1 egg, beaten for egg wash

Instructions:

1. Cut the puff pastry into rounds.
2. Toss the strawberries with sugar and basil, then place the mixture in the center of each pastry round.
3. Fold the edges over the filling, leaving the center exposed.
4. Brush the edges with egg wash.
5. Preheat the air fryer to 360°F (182°C).
6. Cook the galettes for 12-15 minutes until puffed and golden brown.

Cooking Tips:

- Don't overfill the galettes to prevent the juices from spilling out.
- The galettes can be served with a dollop of whipped cream or ice cream.

Air Fryer Mango Sticky Rice Pouches

Prep: 25 mins | Cook: 10 mins | Serves 4

Ingredients:

- 4 sheets rice paper
- 1 ripe mango, thinly sliced
- 1 cup sticky rice, cooked and cooled
- 2 tablespoons coconut cream
- 1 tablespoon sesame seeds
- 1 tablespoon honey or maple syrup

Instructions:

1. Soak a rice paper sheet in warm water until pliable.
2. Place some sticky rice in the center, add a few mango slices, and drizzle with coconut cream.
3. Fold the rice paper over the filling to create a pouch.
4. Preheat the air fryer to 370°F (188°C).
5. Cook the pouches for 8-10 minutes, flipping halfway until crisp.
6. Drizzle with honey or maple syrup and sprinkle with sesame seeds before serving.

Cooking Tips:

- Keep the rice paper moist but not overly wet when wrapping to avoid tearing.
- Serve immediately for the best texture.

Air Fryer Red Velvet Cookie Sandwiches

Prep: 15 mins | Cook: 10 mins | Serves 4

Ingredients:

- 1 box red velvet cake mix
- 2 eggs
- 1/3 cup vegetable oil
- 1/2 cup cream cheese frosting

Instructions:

1. Mix the cake mix, eggs, and vegetable oil to form a cookie dough.
2. Form the dough into small balls and flatten into discs.
3. Preheat the air fryer to 320°F (160°C).
4. Cook the cookie discs for 8-10 minutes.
5. Once cool, sandwich two cookies with cream cheese frosting in between.

Cooking Tips:

- Don't overcook the cookies; they will harden as they cool.
- Let cookies cool completely before adding the frosting to prevent it from melting.

Air Fryer Spiced Apple Turnovers

Prep: 20 mins | Cook: 15 mins | Serves 4

Ingredients:

- 2 apples, peeled and diced
- 1/4 cup brown sugar
- 1 teaspoon ground cinnamon
- 1/2 teaspoon ground nutmeg
- 1 sheet puff pastry, thawed
- 1 egg, beaten for egg wash

Instructions:

1. Toss the diced apples with brown sugar, cinnamon, and nutmeg.
2. Cut the puff pastry into squares and place the apple mixture in the center.
3. Fold the pastry over to form triangles, sealing the edges with a fork.
4. Brush the turnovers with egg wash.
5. Preheat the air fryer to 360°F (182°C).
6. Cook for 12-15 minutes until golden and puffed.

Cooking Tips:

- Ensure the edges are sealed well to prevent the filling from leaking out.
- Serve warm with a scoop of vanilla ice cream or a dusting of powdered sugar.

Appendix 1- COOKING TIMES CHART

POULTRY

Drumsticks	400°F / 200°C	20-25mins
Boneless Chicken Breasts	380°F / 190°C	15-18mins
Boneless Chicken Thighs	400°F / 200°C	15-20mins
Bone-in Chicken Thighs	400°F / 200°C	25-30mins
Wings	400°F / 200°C	15-20mins
Chicken tenders	400°F / 200°C	8-10mins
Boneless Turkey Breasts	360°F / 180°C	45-55mins
Whole Chicken	360°F / 180°C	55-60mins
Cornish game hen	360°F / 180°C	30-35mins
Frozen Chicken Nuggets	400°F / 200°C	10-12mins
Turkey meatballs	400°F / 200°C	8-10mins

SEAFOOD

Salmon	400°F / 200°C	10-12mins
Fish Fillet	400°F / 200°C	8-12mins
Shrimp	400°F / 200°C	8-12mins
Scallops	400°F / 200°C	6-8mins
Tuna Steak	400°F / 200°C	8-10mins
Crab legs	380°F / 190°C	5-7mins
Lobster tail	380°F / 190°C	7-8mins
Frozen Fish Sticks	400°F / 200°C	12mins

VEGETABLES

Brussels Sprouts	400°F / 200°C	8-10mins
Carrots	400°F / 200°C	10-12mins
Asparagus	400°F / 200°C	6-8mins
Green beans	400°F / 200°C	6-8mins
Broccoli	400°F / 200°C	6-8mins
Cauliflower	400°F / 200°C	6-8mins
Whole Potatoes	400°F / 200°C	40-55mins
Potato Wedges	400°F / 200°C	20-25mins
Frozen Fries	400°F / 200°C	15mins
Corn on the cob	400°F / 200°C	10-12mins
Zucchini	400°F / 200°C	6-8mins
Eggplant	400°F / 200°C	6-8mins
Plantains	350°F / 180°C	12-15mins

BEEF

Ribeye steak	400°F / 200°C	12-15mins
Sirloin steak	400°F / 200°C	12-15mins
Round top roast	400°F / 200°C	45-55mins
Steak bites	400°F / 200°C	10-12mins
Meatballs	400°F / 200°C	10-12mins
Burgers	350°F / 180°C	12-15mins
Filet Mignon	400°F / 200°C	15-20mins

PORK

Bacon	400°F / 200°C	10-12mins
Sausages	400°F / 200°C	15-18mins
Pork chops	400°F / 200°C	15-18mins
Ribs	400°F / 200°C	25-30mins
Hot dogs	400°F / 200°C	10mins

FROZEN FOODS

Chicken Nuggets	400°F / 200°C	10-12mins
Turkey meatballs	400°F / 200°C	10-12mins
Salmon	400°F / 200°C	12-15mins
Fish Fillet	400°F / 200°C	12mins
Frozen Popcorn shrimp	400°F / 200°C	8-10mins
Beer Battered Fish	400°F / 200°C	10-12mins
Frozen Fish Sticks	400°F / 200°C	10-12mins
Frozen Crab cakes	400°F / 200°C	10-12mins
Mozarella sticks	360°F / 180°C	7-8mins
Samosa	350°F / 180°C	8-10mins
Taquitos	400°F / 200°C	6-8mins
Egg rolls	350°F / 180°C	8-10mins
Corn dogs	380°F / 190°C	10-12mins
Pigs in a blanket	350°F / 180°C	8-10mins
Cinnamon rolls	330°F / 165°C	8-10mins
Biscuits /Crescent rolls	330°F / 165°C	8mins
Frozen Pizza	380°F / 190°C	6-8mins
Burgers	350°F / 180°C	12-14mins
Tater tots	400°F / 200°C	12-15mins
French Fries	400°F / 200°C	12-15mins

Appendix 2-
MEASUREMENT CONVERSION CHART

VOLUME EQUIVALENTS (DRY)

US STANDARD	METRIC (APPROXIMATE)
1/8 teaspoon	0.5 mL
1/4 teaspoon	1 mL
1/2 teaspoon	2 mL
3/4 teaspoon	4 mL
1 teaspoon	5 mL
1 tablespoon	15 mL
1/4 cup	59 mL
1/2 cup	118 mL
3/4 cup	177 mL
1 cup	235 mL
2 cups	475 mL
3 cups	700 mL
4 cups	1L

WEIGHT EQUIVALENTS

US STANDARD	METRIC (APPROXIMATE)
1 ounce	28 g
2 ounces	57 g
5 ounces	142 g
10 ounces	284 g
15 ounces	425 g
16 ounces	455 g
1.5 pounds	680 g
2 pounds	907 g

VOLUME EQUIVALENTS(LIQUID)

US STANDARD	US STANDARD (US STANDARD)	METRIC (APPROXIMATE)
2 tablespoons	1 fl.oz.	30 mL
1/4 cup	2 fl.oz.	60 mL
1/2 cup	4 fl.oz.	120 mL
1 cup	8 fl.oz.	240 mL
1 1/2 cup	12 fl.oz.	355 mL
2 cups or 1 pint	16 fl.oz.	475 mL
4 cups or 1 quart	32 fl.oz.	1 L
1 gallon	128 fl.oz.	4 L

TEMPERATURES EQUIVALENTS

FAHRENHEIT(F)	CELSIUS(C)
225 °F	107 °C
250 °F	120 °C
275 °F	135 °C
300 °F	150 °C
325 °F	160 °C
350 °F	180 °C
375 °F	190 °C
400 °F	205 °C
425 °F	220 °C
450 °F	235 °C
475 °F	245 °C
500 °F	260°C

Made in the USA
Las Vegas, NV
28 July 2024